# PRECISION TRIM CARPENTRY

# precision trim
# CARPENTRY

**Rick Williams**

**POPULAR WOODWORKING BOOKS**
CINCINNATI, OHIO
www.popularwoodworking.com

## READ THIS IMPORTANT SAFETY NOTICE

## metric conversion chart

| TO CONVERT | TO | MULTIPLY BY |
|---|---|---|
| Inches | Centimeters | 2.54 |
| Centimeters | Inches | 0.4 |
| Feet | Centimeters | 30.5 |
| Centimeters | Feet | 0.03 |
| Yards | Meters | 0.9 |
| Meters | Yards | 1.1 |
| Sq. Inches | Sq. Centimeters | 6.45 |
| Sq. Centimeters | Sq. Inches | 0.16 |
| Sq. Feet | Sq. Meters | 0.09 |
| Sq. Meters | Sq. Feet | 10.8 |
| Sq. Yards | Sq. Meters | 0.8 |
| Sq. Meters | Sq. Yards | 1.2 |
| Pounds | Kilograms | 0.45 |
| Kilograms | Pounds | 2.2 |
| Ounces | Grams | 28.4 |
| Grams | Ounces | 0.035 |

**Precision Trim Carpentry.** Copyright © 2003 by Rick Williams. Printed and bound in China. All rights reserved. No part of this book may be reproduced in any form or by any electronic or mechanical means including information storage and retrieval systems without permission in writing from the publisher, except by a reviewer, who may quote brief passages in a review. Published by Popular Woodworking Books, an imprint of F&W Publications, Inc., 4700 East Galbraith Road, Cincinnati, Ohio, 45236. First edition.

Visit our Web site at www.popularwoodworking.com for information on more resources for woodworkers.

Other fine Popular Woodworking Books are available from your local bookstore or direct from the publisher.

07   06   05   04     5   4   3

**Library of Congress Cataloging-in-Publication Data**

Williams, Rick,
  Precision trim carpentry / by Rick Williams.
    p. cm.
Includes bibliographical references and index.
  ISBN 1-55870-636-4 (pbk. : alk. paper)
  1. Trim carpentry.  I. Title.
  TH5695 .W55 2003
  694'.6--dc21

                              2002152358

ACQUISITIONS EDITOR: Jim Stack
EDITOR: Jennifer Ziegler
DESIGNER: Brian Roeth
LAYOUT ARTIST: Tari Sasser
PRODUCTION COORDINATOR: Mark Griffin

This book is dedicated to my wife Dee, my son Ryan, and my daughter Rikki, for without them I'm not me.

## About the Author

Rick Williams is a general building contractor and custom cabinetmaker by trade. The majority of his work is additions and remodels. Over the years he has learned a few tricks and discovered others about how to dress up your home without breaking the bank.

## Acknowledgements

First, as in my last book, I would like to thank my 14-year-old son, Ryan, who is my personal editor and writer. Without his help I would still be slowly pecking, one finger at a time, on the computer keyboard to write this book.

I would also like to thank my editor, Jim Stack, and all the rest of the folks at Popular Woodworking Books who have worked so hard to put this book together. They truly make my job easy.

I owe a special thanks to my 11-year-old daughter, Rikki, for waiting so patiently for me to finish this book before building her desk that she designed herself.

Many thanks to Ellen Huntoon for letting me photograph her new home during construction for this book, and for letting me come back and photograph the finished product after she moved in.

My appreciation goes out to Bob De Marco and Traci Meyers at Top Quality Insulation and Fireplaces in Valley Spring, California, for supplying the fireplace in the built-in bookcase. Many thanks also to Rich Muncy at Heron Door in Sonora, California, for the interior divided light doors, and Randy Dominick at Randy's Door and Trim in Murphys, California, for supplying all the pre-hung doors and trim used in this book. I can't say enough about using local small businesses in your projects; they are a great source of help and knowledge. Thanks guys.

# table of contents

# project kids: a labor of love

MORE THAN FIVE YEARS AGO, RICK Williams was a scoutleader for his son's Cub Scout pack. All of their Scout meetings took place in Rick's wood-shop, a room that fascinated the group of boys. The pride and satisfaction the group seemed to acquire from building small projects inspired Rick to build his own personal "field of dreams." Investing their own time and money, Rick and his wife, DeEtta, purchased a 25'-long trailer and outfitted it with nine small workbenches. Calling it Project Kids, Rick took his trailer on the road to local elementary schools, senior care centers and other locations. The focus of Project Kids is on disabled or handicapped children, disadvantaged children, continuing education students and senior citizens at care facilities. The goal of Project Kids is to provide kids of all ages and disabilities the opportunity to realize for themselves the joy, pride and sense of accomplishment in building something with their own hands. Rick offers this service for free to any child or adult who can benefit from it, and he organizes sessions around his busy work schedule. The Williamses invest their own money into Project Kids; some minimal donations have been offered to them, as well. Some day, Rick hopes to be sponsored by a corporation in order to continue his work with Project Kids and to expand the service area and capabilities of Project Kids.

All of the wooden toys that are created by participants at the nine Project Kids workbench stations are partially precut and prepped by Rick and his volunteers. Rick wants the participants to learn something about woodworking, but he also wants to be sure each child is able to finish their project and experience the feeling of self-sufficiency and pride that comes with a completed toy. "They cut out the final pieces themselves, under my supervision, of course, and then they do the drilling and sanding." Each workstation in the trailer is equipped with a hammer, a saw, a screwdriver, a square, a hand drill, a sanding block and safety glasses. Rick has circulated the Project Kids trailer throughout Calaveras County in north-central California, where he lives; but he has bigger dreams. He's had requests to bring his trailer to Los Angeles, San Francisco

and elsewhere in his home state. Each time he offers a session, he receives two or three requests from other organizations. Although it's called Project Kids, Rick often offers his traveling workshop to senior care centers. "I've had kids from age 2 through age 92," he says. His most difficult obstacle in sharing Project Kids is his day job as a contractor; scheduling weekday sessions is often a conflict, but he fits in every appointment he possibly can. "The kids' energy is boundless, and that's my reward," he says. "The experience of Project Kids is just so awesome; I could talk about it for days!" Rick welcomes any queries about Project Kids; he can be contacted at:

Project Kids
P.O. Box 1285
Murphys, California 95247
Fax: 209-728-3769
bodee@sonnet.com.

# INTRODUCTION

In this book I will show you how to do most of the interior woodwork needed to complete that remodel or addition to your home. Whether you just want to install a new door and a little crown moulding in the living room, or complete that interior remodel with wainscot and hardwood flooring, the step-by-step photos will show you the way. The techniques are easy and you'll be amazed at the finished results, not to mention the increase in value to your home. I hope you enjoy dressing up your home as much as I do mine.

  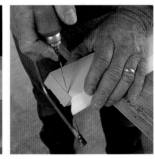

# CHAPTER ONE

# wood-cased window trim

On most houses, the windows are trimmed with drywall on two sides and the top, with a wooden windowsill on the bottom. A nice upgrade is a full wood-cased window. There are many different options on how to trim a window. I will show one quick and easy option, but feel free to elaborate on the final trim that goes around your window.

Measure and cut to length the top
and bottom jamb pieces.

Remove the wooden windowsill and drywall
from around the window. Fill any gaps with
insulation.

Using No. 8 finish nails, install the top and bottom jamb pieces. Put
shims between the house's window framing and the jamb as necessary
to keep the jamb aligned with the window frame. Bundles of tapered
shims are available at most home-improvement centers.

Measure and cut the side jamb pieces to fit
between the top and bottom jambs.

Sometimes you'll encounter gaps after the jambs have been installed. Use a shim to press the top piece against the side piece to close the gap.

Attach the side jambs with No. 8 nails. If necessary, use shims to keep the jambs even with the window frame.

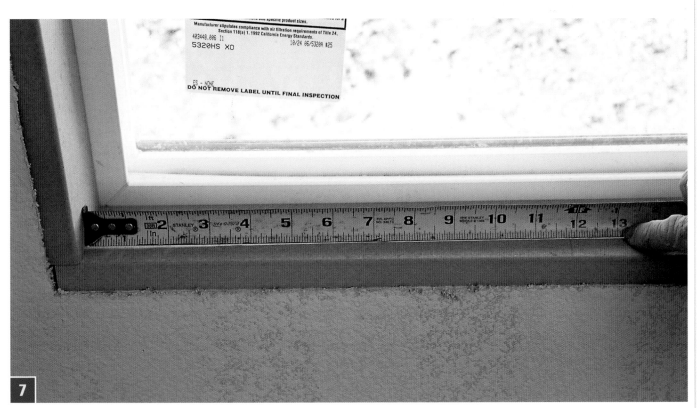

Now you can install the window trim. Measure the distance between the sides at the top and bottom of the window, then add ½". When the trim is cut and installed, this will create a reveal from the edge of the trim to the inside edge of the jamb.

**8**

Cut the trim on a 45° angle at each end. Remember, the short distance between the miter cuts is the measurement you took in the previous step. Using No. 4 finish nails, attach the bottom and top pieces of trim as shown to create the ¼" reveal.

**9**

Occasionally the drywall may have bulges. Use your hammer to gently tap the bulges flat before installing the trim.

**10**

After tapping with your hammer, you may need to trim the excess drywall from the edge with a utility knife.

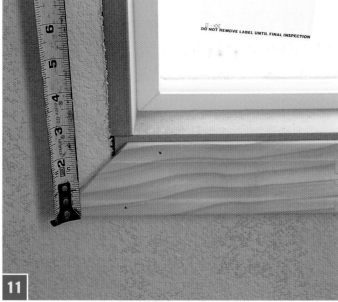

**11**

Measure for the side piece of trim at the longest point of the angles. Repeat this process for the other side.

**12**

Nail the two side pieces in place to complete the cased window trim. If necessary, trim the miters so they create a tight joint.

**13**

This window trim was painted off-white, a nice accent to the pastel green walls.

**14**

## CONSTRUCTION TIPS

▥ If you want a painted window frame, I recommend using an inexpensive material for the jambs, such as medium-density fiberboard (MDF). This material is easy to work with, takes paint well and can be purchased at any home-improvement store.

This type of window trim adds a great deal of beauty to any ordinary window. Shutters can be easily attached to the jambs if desired.

# CHAPTER TWO

# wood-cased openings between rooms

In many homes, the openings between rooms — such as dining room to kitchen and hallway to living room — have not been given the attention they deserve. An easy way to dress up these openings is to case them in wood trim. You can select from many different styles of trim. I have chosen one popular style called 21" colonial. Feel free to choose the style you prefer; the technique for casing the opening remains the same.

**1**

Before installing the jambs, scrape any excess drywall flush with the wood frame.

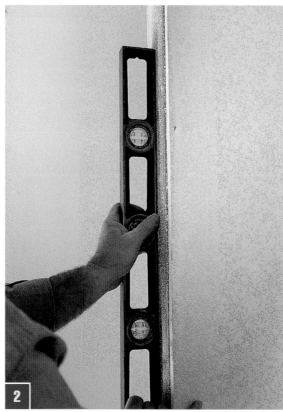

**2**

Using your level, check to see if the wood framing is plumb. Use the top and bottom bubble levels for this. When both bubbles are centered, you've found plumb. (You will have a little bit of play between the jamb and the wood framing for adjustments and shimming when installing the cased opening.)

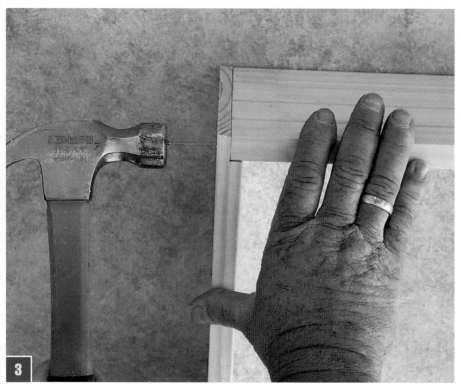

**3**

You can purchase standard $4\frac{1}{2}$"-wide door jamb kits at your local home-improvement store. (Most interior walls are made of 2×4s, which are actually $3\frac{1}{2}$" wide, with $\frac{1}{2}$" of drywall on each side. This totals $4\frac{1}{2}$" thick.) These kits have a precut dado on the two side jambs to receive the top jamb, as shown in the photo. After measuring and cutting the top and side jambs to length, assemble them using No. 4 finish nails.

4

After setting the jamb assembly in the opening, use shims to plumb the side jambs and level the top jamb. Nail the jamb to the wall framing using No. 8 finish nails. If you use shims, install the nails under the shims. This will keep the jamb flat and hold the shims in place.

## CONSTRUCTION TIPS

▩ Note that the nails used to hold the jambs in place are located below the shims. This will allow adjustments to the shims and ensure the jamb is pulled tightly to the shims. If you put nails farther away from the shims, the jamb will become bowed because of the pressure of the nails.

When all is as you want it, set the nails to ensure that the jambs will stay in place.

Use your utility knife to cut any excess off of the shims.

**7** Cut the casing trim at a 45° angle, with the shortest point ¼" longer than the inside corner of the jamb, as shown by the pencil lines.

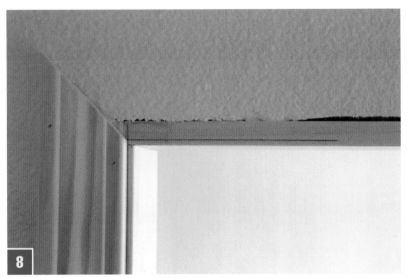

**8** Use No. 4 finish nails to attach the trim to the jambs. Maintain the ¼" reveal around the opening.

**9** Install the trim on both sides of the opening.

# CHAPTER THREE

# closet bypass doors

The two main types of closet doors are bypass doors and bifold doors. Bifold doors allow full access to the closet, but are a little more difficult to install and are not quite as durable for heavy use. Bypass doors are more suited to places like kids' bedrooms, where the closet doors are opened and closed frequently. They still allow plenty of access to the closet by simply sliding them to one side or the other.

Before installing the bypass doors, scrape any excess drywall until it's flush with the wood frame.

Using your level, check to see if the wood framing is plumb. You will have a little bit of play between the bypass jamb and the wood framing for adjustments and shimming when installing the door.

# picking the right trim

Your house framing may be out of plumb quite a bit. Use shims as required to keep the door jambs plumb. Most standard door trim will cover these problems, but occasionally you may need to use a wider door trim to cover the gap. Check a few of the walls that you are working on to see if they are plumb. If they are out more than 1" from top to bottom, you might want to consider picking a wider style of door trim at the beginning of the project. This will allow you to cover any irregularities and make the project look more consistent.

If you are installing bypass closet doors over carpet, it is a good idea to use a $\frac{3}{8}$" spacer underneath the bypass door jamb during installation. When installation is complete, remove the spacers. This allows clearance between the bottom of the doors and the carpet.

If you are ambitious, you may cut all the jamb pieces yourself for the bypass doors, but my personal preference is to buy the parts from a local door shop. All the parts should be precut and ready for assembly. Lay out the parts as shown.

Hold the side jambs to the top jamb with the J-hook side of the track to the inside of the closet. Notice the notch in the top front of the side jamb. This is to accept the wood skirt that hides the metal track from view.

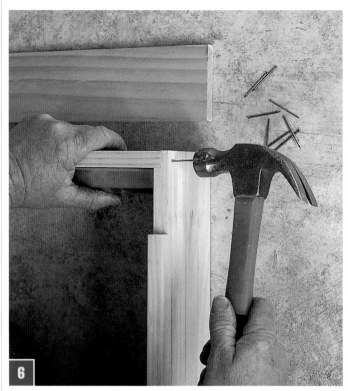

**6**

Nail the side jambs to the head jamb, using No. 4 finish nails.

**7**

Nail the wood skirt in the notch with No. 4 finish nails.

**8**

After positioning the assembled jamb in the closet opening (and on top of the ³⁄₈" spacers, if necessary), use shims at the top of the jamb assembly and center the assembly in the closet door opening. Using No. 8 finish nails, nail the jambs to the frame just underneath the shims. This will allow you to adjust your shims if necessary.

Using one 2"-long wood screw, screw the head jamb to the closet frame to remove any sag caused by the weight of the doors.

Install the inside door first by tilting the top of the door away from you and hooking the wheels on the top of the door onto the track farthest away from you. (Your local door shop may preinstall the wheel hardware onto the doors for you.) Repeat the process for the outside door and its track.

When the doors are closed, make sure that the predrilled closet door pulls are on the outside of the closet and set on the edges of the doors that are next to the side jambs.

After sliding the outside closet door closed, use shims to adjust the bottom of the side jamb until it rests against the door.

Slide the outside closet door open and nail the side jamb to the closet frame just below the shims using No. 8 finish nails.

Slide the outside closet door closed again and, moving up the jamb about one-third of the way, use shims to adjust the side jambs to the door.

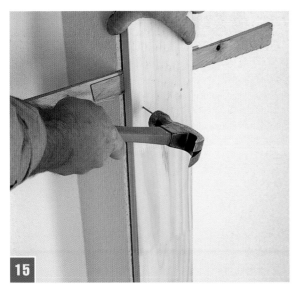

**15**

Slide the outside closet door open again and nail the side jamb to the closet frame just below the shims using No. 8 finish nails.

Moving up the jamb another one-third of the way, use shims to adjust the jamb to the door, then nail the jamb to the closet frame, using No. 8 finish nails just below the shims.

**16**

**17**

Set the nails to hold the jamb in place.

Using your utility knife, cut off any of the excess shims. Repeat this shimming process on the other side jamb.

Cut your door trim at a 45° angle at the shortest point, ½" shorter than the outside corner of the door jamb.

Using No. 4 finish nails, nail the trim onto the side jamb and wood frame, maintaining a ¼" reveal all the way down the side jamb. Install the other side trim parts outside and inside the closet.

Measure and cut the outside and the inside top trim at a 45° angle on both ends, then attach with No. 4 finish nails.

## CONSTRUCTION TIPS

▓ When installing bypass doors over carpeting, install a ³⁄₈" x 6" x 6" wooden spacer in the center of the closet door opening on the floor. Install the carpet padding around the block, and install the carpeting over the block. Then attach the closet door guide on top of the carpeted block. This is to keep the door guide from sinking too far into the carpet and padding.

After you have finished the installation and painting, you will appreciate the usability and appearance of these bypass doors for years to come.

# CHAPTER FOUR

# closet bifold doors

As noted in the previous chapter, the two main types of closet doors are bypass doors and bifold doors. Bypass are the easier to install, but only half of the closet can be accessed at one time. With bifold doors, the entire closet can be opened at once. This type of closet door works well for a hall storage closet or utility closet, as well as a wardrobe.

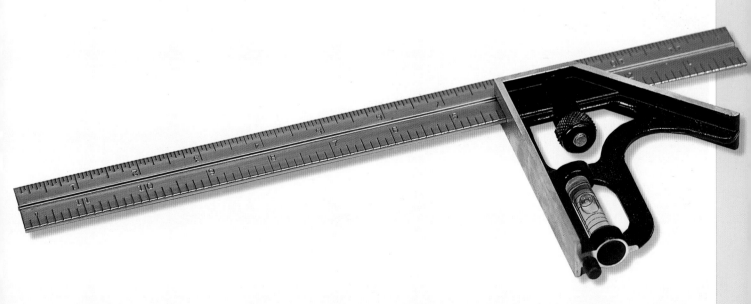

Before installing bifold doors, scrape any excess drywall flush with the wood frame.

Using your level, check to see if the wood framing is plumb. You will have a little bit of play between the bifold jamb and the wood framing for adjustments and shimming when installing the door.

## CONSTRUCTION TIPS

▐ Note that the nails used to hold the jambs in place are located below the shims. This will allow adjustments to the shims and ensure the jamb is pulled tightly to the shims. If you put nails farther away from the shims, the jamb will become bowed because of the pressure of the nails.

At your local home-improvement store or door shop, purchase a bifold door and framing kit that will fit your closet opening. Nail together the side jambs to the top jamb and set it into place, centering the jamb in the opening using shims. Using No. 8 finish nails, nail the top of each side jamb to the wood frame, then, using your level, plumb the jamb down to the floor. Use shims at the bottom of the jamb as necessary.

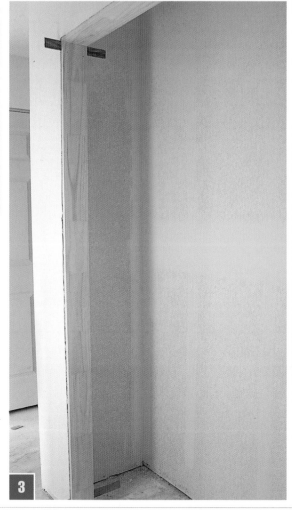

Open the hardware package that came with the bifold door and lay out all the pieces for ease of assembly.

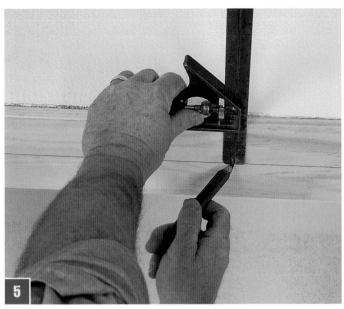

Using a combination square and a pencil, draw a center line across the entire length of the top jamb.

Attach the door guide track to the center line of the top jamb, using the screws provided.

Attach the door bottom pivot bracket to the center of the jamb, using the screws provided. Note: If the door is being installed over carpet, install a ⅜"-thick spacer underneath the bracket to allow for the thickness of the carpet and padding.

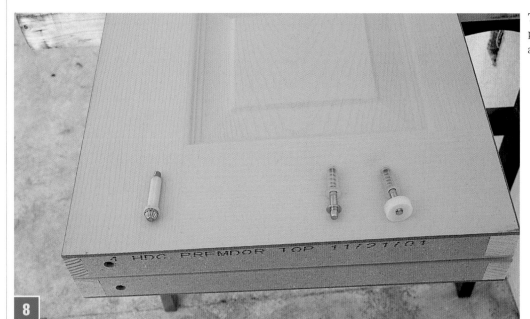

The bifold door will come with predrilled holes for the hardware, as shown in the photo.

Follow the hardware installation instructions when installing the top pivot pin. Note: The hardware for the top of the door is spring-loaded. When tapping the hardware in with your hammer, hold down the spring with the centering door guide that came in the hardware package.

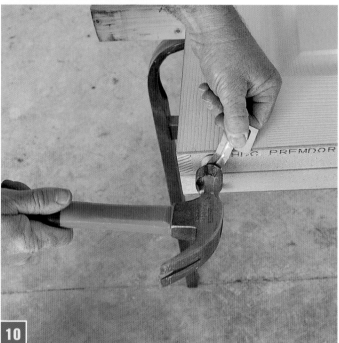

Install the top guide roller wheel in the same manner as the top pivot pin.

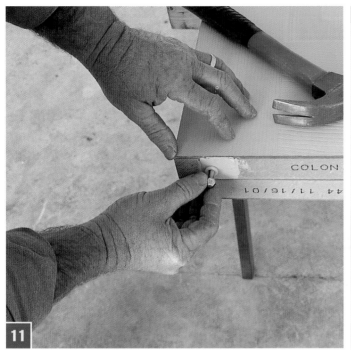

**11** Position the bottom pivot pin in the predrilled hole in the bottom of the door. Note: The bottom hardware is not spring-loaded.

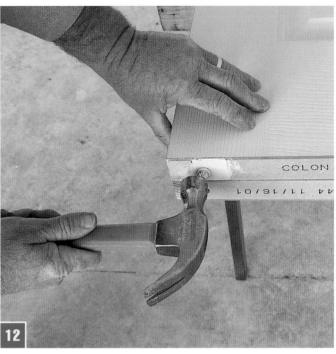

**12** Tap in the bottom pivot pin with your hammer.

**13**

Install the bifold doors by putting the hardware on the top of the door into the top track, raising the door and positioning the bottom pivot pin onto the pivot bracket.

Adjust the bottom pivot pin in or out to allow for clearance between the door and the side jamb for opening and closing. Next, adjust the door up or down by turning the pivot pin to allow $\frac{7}{8}$" between the top of the door and the top jamb.

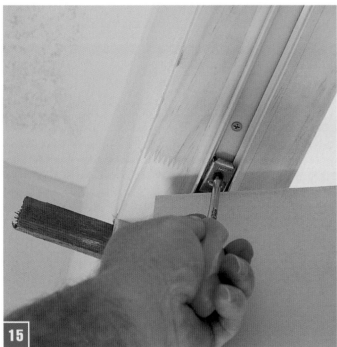

Using a Phillips screwdriver, adjust the top pivot bracket in or out from the side jamb. This allows for clearance between the door and the side jamb for opening and closing the doors.

Shim and nail the side jamb as necessary to maintain an equal margin between the door edge and side jamb.

Set all nails to hold the jambs securely.

Using a utility knife, trim off the excess shim shingles.

Cut your door trim at a 45° angle, $\frac{1}{4}$" longer than the inside corner of the door jamb at the shortest point, as shown by the pencil lines on the jamb. Repeat this process for the outside and inside jambs.

Using No. 4 finish nails, nail the trim onto the side jamb and wood framing, maintaining the $\frac{1}{4}$" margin all the way down the side jamb. Repeat this process for the other three sides.

Measure and cut the outside and the inside top trim at a 45° angle on both ends, then attach with No. 4 finish nails.

Use $\frac{3}{4}$" quarter-round trim to finish the door opening. Cut a 45° angle at the top of the trim and nail it to the side jamb, using No. 4 finish nails. Maintain a $\frac{1}{8}$" clearance between the trim and the door. Repeat this process for the other side.

**23** Cut and install the top quarter-round trim. This will hide the top door track.

When you're finished, paint the doors so they blend into your room or hallway. **24**

**25** The accessibility of the items in the closet make bifold doors a great option.

## CONSTRUCTION TIPS

▨ Before installing carpet, remove the bottom pivot bracket, leaving the $^3/_8$"-thick spacer block. Install the carpet pad around the block, and the carpet over the block, then reinstall the spacer bracket over the carpet.

# CHAPTER FIVE

# baseboards

**B**aseboards are available in many types for different styles of homes. I will illustrate how to install one popular style that will look nice in many different homes, but the technique can be applied to any style and size of baseboard. You can also make elaborate baseboards by combining multiple pieces. Feel free to design your own style of baseboard to suit your tastes.

**1**

Baseboards can be installed using two different methods. One method is to measure the wall, corner to corner, and cut the baseboard to that length with a 45° angle at each end. With this method, though, when nailing the baseboard to the wall, the gap has a tendency to open up, as seen in this photo.

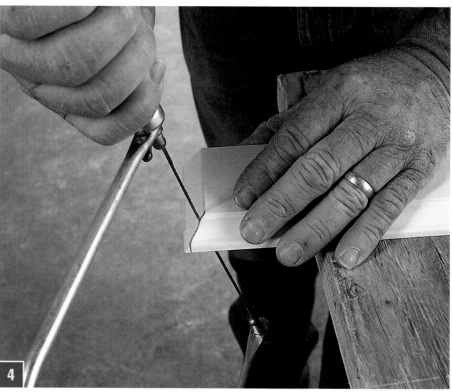

**2**

I prefer the other method, which is to cut the first piece of baseboard at a 90° angle, wall to wall (or in this photo, door casing to wall).

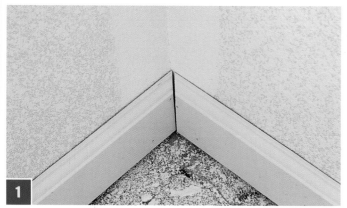

**3**

Measure the next piece of baseboard from wall to wall. Cut a 45° angle on the end of the baseboard that will connect with the first piece of baseboard. Make a square cut on the opposite end. (The length of this piece is measured from the long part of the 45° angle to the square cut on the opposite end.)

**4**

Using the 45° cut as a pattern line, use a coping saw and cut along the edge of the 45° bevel. Hold the saw at a slight angle to create an undercut.

## CONSTRUCTION TIPS

▓ When installing a baseboard, some installations require the bottom to be at different heights, such as for carpets. I use ³/₈"-thick spacers to hold the baseboard up off the floor to allow carpet to be tucked underneath.

**5** Cut the contour of the baseboard first, then make the straight cut.

**6** This is the finished cut.

**7** When positioning the baseboard, put the square cut against the opposite wall and slide the baseboard into position as shown. Note that there is no gap after the baseboard has been nailed on.

# CHAPTER SIX

# paint-grade wainscot

A fun way to add a special flair to your home is to install wainscot in your hallway, entry or any room where you want to add a formal look and feel. Wainscot is easy to decorate and can be done in a paint-grade or a stain-grade version to match many different styles. In this chapter I will show an easy way to install a painted wainscot in your home.

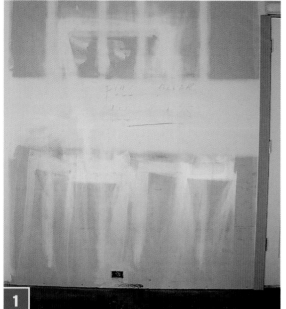

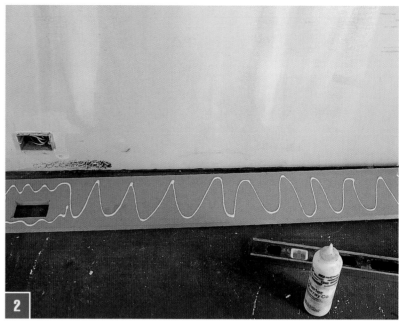

When picking the walls where you want to install wainscot, electrical outlets or other obstacles may be in your way. You will have two choices; one is to lay out your panels so that the outlets will fall into the middle of the panels. This will affect the uniformity of the wainscot. The other option is to have the outlets moved to the lower portion of the wall by a qualified electrician, as I have done.

I like to use ³⁄₄"-thick MDF for painted wainscot. It is stable, smooth and easily painted. Measure the length of the wall where you are installing wainscot; in my case I went from the inside corner of the wall to the edge of the door casing. I typically make my bottom rail ³⁄₄" thick by 7" tall. This will allow room for the electrical outlets. After cutting out the holes for outlets, apply a cabinet-grade glue to the bottom rail.

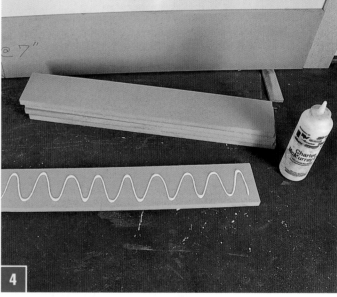

Shim the bottom rail level and nail it to the framing studs using No. 8 finish nails.

Stiles are typically ³⁄₄" thick by 4" wide by 24" tall.

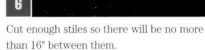

Cut enough stiles so there will be no more than 16" between them.

Apply glue to the back of the stile and to the top of the rail where the stile will go. Then nail the glued stile to the inside corner of the wall using No. 8 finish nails.

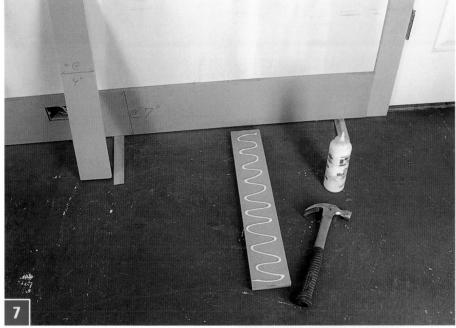

Use your level and mark a plumb line where each stile will be located. After marking the stile locations on the wall, apply glue to the backs of the remaining stiles.

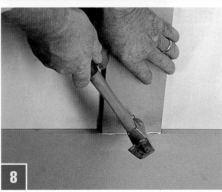

After applying glue to the top of the bottom rail where the stiles will go, nail the stiles to the wall using No. 8 finish nails. Note: The nails for the stiles will probably catch only drywall, not the wall framing. This is fine, because when dry, the glue will hold the stile in place.

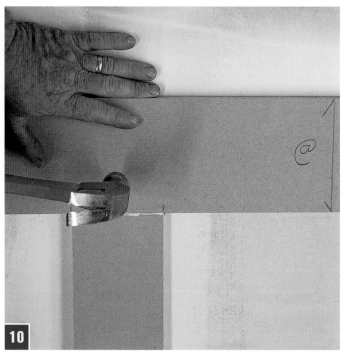

Position the top rail on top of the stiles. Using No. 8 finish nails, attach the rail to the wall. Nail into framing where possible.

**9**

Cut the top rail to length, which is typically $\frac{3}{4}$" thick by 5" wide. Apply glue to the top of the stiles and to the edge of the door casing where the top rail will meet the casing.

**10**

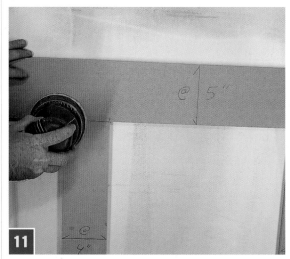

**11**

After the glue has dried, sand the joints smooth.

**12**

I create a $\frac{1}{8}$" step with a $\frac{1}{4}$" roundover on the inside edges of the framework, using a router and a $\frac{1}{4}$" roundover bit. Set the height of the router so the router bit will cut the $\frac{1}{8}$" step. Make sure the tip of the router bit does not touch the wall.

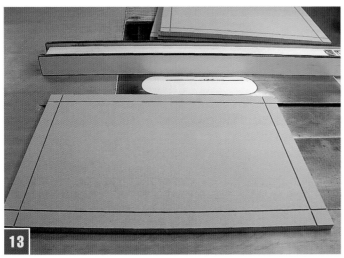

**13**

**14**

After measuring (deduct $\frac{1}{16}$" from the width and height of the opening to allow for expansion and contraction) when cutting the pieces for the panels, set your table saw fence to $1\frac{3}{8}$" and adjust your blade height to $\frac{1}{8}$" high. Cut grooves in each panel as shown in the photo.

Set your table saw blade to a 10° angle and adjust to $1\frac{3}{8}$" high. Set your saw fence to allow the inside of the saw blade to line up with the back of the $\frac{1}{8}$" notch that you have already cut. Cut a bevel on all four edges of each panel.

**15**

Sand out any saw marks on the panels.

**16**

Apply a liberal amount of glue to the backs of the panels.

**17**

Place the panels into the wainscot assembly and attach them to the wall using No. 8 finish nails. If possible, nail into the wall studs.

**18**

I use base-cap moulding to finish the top of the wainscot. You can purchase base-cap moulding at your local home-improvement store. I'm using preprimed paint-grade base-cap moulding.

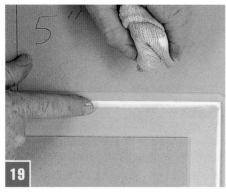

**19**

Caulk the gaps between the rails, stiles and panels using a good paint-grade caulking.

**20**

One of the most important steps in doing a paint-grade version of any wainscot is the caulking. Be sure to caulk all of the joints and seams. When painted, the wainscot appears as a seamless part of the wall.

**21**

A paint-grade wainscot is a great accent for any home.

## CONSTRUCTION TIPS

▓ For a paint-grade wainscot, I recommend using medium-density fiberboard (MDF). It is inexpensive, easy to work with and takes paint well.

# CHAPTER SEVEN

# stain-grade wainscot

Wainscot is a great accent to any home. In the previous chapter I showed how to construct an easy paint-grade wainscot. In this chapter I will show how to make a stain-grade version. The stain-grade version is a bit more difficult and time-consuming, but if you are willing to go for it, rest assured you will be pleased with the final product.

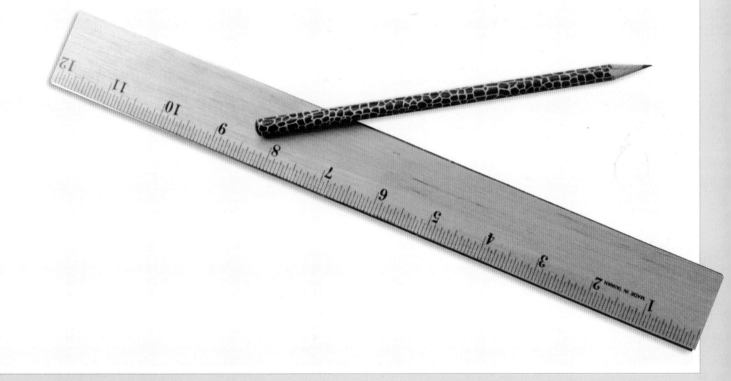

When measuring the walls where you want to install wainscot, electrical outlets or other obstacles may be in your way. You will have two choices; one is to lay out your panels so that the outlets will fall into the middle of the panels. This will affect the uniformity of the wainscot. The other option is to have the outlets moved to the lower portion of the wall by a qualified electrician, as I have done.

After determining the layout of the wainscot, with panels typically not more than 16" wide by ¾" thick, the bottom rail 7" high, the top rail 5" high and stiles 4" wide, cut all the rail and stile pieces out of ¾"-thick stock. I drill two pocket holes in the ends of each stile on the back side.

Glue and screw the rails and stiles together using No. 6 × 1¼"-long pocket-hole drilling jig screws.

After the rail and stile frames are assembled, position the frames on the walls. Shim as needed to level the frames. Then, mark and cut holes as needed for electrical outlets. Fit any corner joints using a sander or block plane.

After you have dry fit all the panel assemblies together, remove the assemblies from the wall.

Sand the face of the panel assemblies smooth.

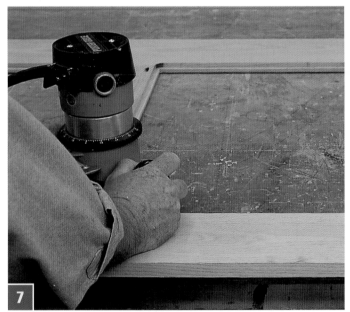

Using your router and a ⅜" rabbeting bit set ⅜" deep, rout the inside of the back panel assemblies, as shown in the photo.

I use a ¼" roundover router bit to rout the inside front edges of the panel assemblies, as shown in the photo.

**9**

Using your finish sander, sand the front of the panel assemblies.

**10**

Glue together smaller stock to make the panels. I drill pocket holes in the backs of the boards. Note: Make sure the screws are at least 2" in from the ends of the panels.

**11**

Glue and screw the boards together to make the panels using No. 6 × 1¼"-long pocket-hole drilling jig screws. I've found this is a quick and effective way to make panels without having to use clamps.

**12**

Cut the panels ⅛" smaller than the width and height of the rabbeted openings in the back of the frame assemblies. Set your table saw blade to ⅛" high and the fence to 1⅜", and cut four grooves in the face of the panels, as shown.

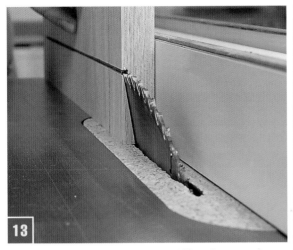

Then, set your table saw blade to a 10° angle and adjust to $1\frac{3}{8}$" high. Set the saw fence to allow the inside of the saw blade to line up with the back of the $\frac{1}{8}$" groove that you have already cut. Cut a bevel on all four edges of each panel, as shown in the photo.

Use your belt sander to round the corners of the panels to fit the radii of the rabbets in the back of the frame assemblies.

Using your finish sander, sand out saw marks on the edges of the panels and sand the faces of the panels smooth.

Apply a little glue in the rabbet of the panel assembly. If you live in an area where seasonal changes are drastic, apply glue in the top and bottom rabbets only. This will allow the panel to move with the seasons.

Set the panels into the rabbets and nail into place using $^5/_8$"-long brads angled into the rabbet.

Reinstall the completed wainscot assembly on the wall using No. 8 finish nails.

Finish the top of the wainscot with a piece of $^3/_4$" × $1^1/_8$" solid stock with a $^1/_4$" radius on the top and bottom edges. Cut to length and nail it to the top of the wainscot assembly using No. 8 finish nails.

Use $\frac{1}{2}$" quarter-round moulding to finish the top of the wainscot cap.
(This quarter-round has already been stained to color.)

## CONSTRUCTION TIPS

▧ If you are installing a stained wainscot over a fancy paint or wallpaper, stain the trim pieces that come in contact with the paint or wallpaper prior to installing them for a no-mess installation.

Stained wainscot adds a warm look and feel to any room.

# CHAPTER EIGHT

# replacement doors

When remodeling your home, something you might consider is replacing your interior doors with a new style that will better accent your room. In this case we chose to replace a pair of painted six-panel doors with a pair of light-oak divided doors to add a more open feel to our home.

Before removing the doors, measure the width of both doors together when closed. I recommend purchasing the new style of doors at a local door shop. The door shop will trim the doors to fit your opening.

Using a nail set and hammer, remove the hinge pins. Note: Use caution not to let the door fall when removing the last pin from each side.

Using a pair of sawhorses as a table, place the new door on the sawhorses with the hinged side of the door facing down. Place the old door on top of the new door (making sure the door tops are on the same ends) and clamp together. Using a square, transfer the hinge locations to the new door.

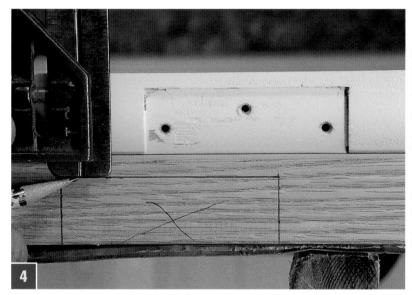

Unclamp the doors and slide the old door back a little. Adjust your square to the hinge height on the old door and transfer that line to the new door.

Using a hammer and chisel, cut a mortise to the required hinge depth.

**6**

After installing all the hinges and hanging the new doors in the jambs, close the doors and check the alignments. In my case the tops of the doors are out of alignment. Hold a straightedge from jamb to jamb and draw a trim line on the doors.

**7**

Remove each door from the jamb, place it on the sawhorses and clamp down.
Using a belt sander, trim the door as required.

We decided to use ball catches to allow both doors to be opened at the same time. Mark the location on the top of each door opposite the hinge side and install the ball catches per the manufacturer's instructions. If you prefer a standard doorknob latch system, the local door shop can prep the doors for you.

## CONSTRUCTION TIPS

▓ If you are using a standard doorknob latch on a pair of doors, an astragal (it acts as a doorstop in this case) is required between the doors. This can be purchased at a local door shop.

After hanging the doors back on the jambs, close them and mark the locations for the striker plates on the head jamb. Using a hammer and a chisel, cut the mortises for the strike plates, then install the strike plates.

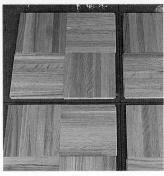

# CHAPTER NINE

# parquet flooring

**M**any types of flooring are available today, from carpeting to tile to imitation wood. They all have their advantages, but it is hard to beat a real hardwood floor in your home. Oak parquet flooring is one of the more popular types and, fortunately, relatively inexpensive and easy to install. You can purchase unfinished or prefinished parquet. I chose the prefinished type to cut back on the mess. The factory finish holds up very well.

**1**

Using your belt sander, sand smooth any
uneven places on your floor.

**2**

Parquet flooring comes in 12" × 12" tiles. Measure and divide your
room to allow for equal amounts of partial parquet tiles on each side.
For example, if your room measured 12' 9" × 14' 3", you would have
$4\frac{1}{2}$" of partial tile on each side in the width and $1\frac{1}{2}$" on each side in
the length. Draw a line on the floor parallel with one wall at 2' plus the
partial parquet tile's width from the wall.

**3**

Measure the room in the opposite direction and divide in the same manner. Lay a straightedge
on the line you drew previously. Then, lay a framing square against the straightedge and draw
a line at a 90° angle to the first line at 2' plus the partial parquet tile's width from the wall.

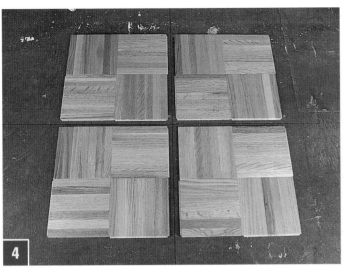

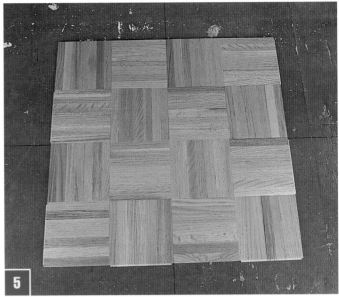

Before spreading any glue, place four parquet tiles on the floor at the intersection of the lines.

Slide the tiles together and check the lines on the floor with the tiles. The lines and joints of the squares need to line up perfectly.

Using the trowel and glue recommended on the parquet instructions, spread only enough glue for a few tiles, being careful to follow your layout lines. Make cutouts in the parquet for vents before placing the tiles in the glue!

It is recommended that you leave $\frac{1}{2}$" for expansion and contraction of the tiles at wall edges and around any brick for fireplaces or other fixed obstacles.

Using a baseboard of your choice, trim the edges of the parquet to walls and cabinets. At the joint of the brick hearth and floor, I used a $\frac{1}{2}$"-thick by 1"-wide moulding glued and nailed to the floor. If the baseboard is unfinished, use masking tape to cover the edges of the parquet tiles, bricks and cabinets prior to applying the finish.

Apply a floor finish to the trim compatible with the prefinished parquet floor, typically a water-based polyurethane finish.

It is hard to beat the warm wood appearance of an oak parquet floor.

## CONSTRUCTION TIPS

▮▮▮ When doing any power sanding, be sure to use the dust collection bag. Sanding dust is irritating to your lungs and throat, not to mention hard to clean from the room.

**CHAPTER TEN**

# interior house doors

When doing any remodel or addition, you will probably have to install an interior house door. In this chapter I will show how to easily install a standard interior door and jamb that can be purchased at your local home-improvement store or door shop.

Using your level, check to see that the door frame is plumb.

Using a scraping tool, scrape away any excess drywall from the wall framing lumber.

Use $^3/_8$" spacing blocks to temporarily hold the door jamb off the floor during installation.

**4**

Before purchasing a door to be installed, determine the direction of the door's swing. It will be a right-hand swing or a left-hand swing. Different parts of the country interchange these terms, so check with the home-improvement store or door shop for the correct swing that you need.

**5**

If you purchase a door from a door shop, it will come prehinged to the assembled jambs, and the door jamb will be tacked to the door with nails on the doorknob side of the jamb. You must remove these nails before installation.

**6**

Leaving the door hinged to the jamb, install the door into the door frame opening, setting the door jamb onto the ³⁄₈" spacer blocks.

Center the jamb in the door frame opening flush with the drywall on each side. Put a shim at the top of the jamb. Nail the jamb just below the shim and above the top hinge using No. 8 finish nails.

7

8

Repeat on the doorknob side of the jamb.

## CONSTRUCTION TIPS

■ When installing bypass doors over carpeting, install a ³⁄₈" x 6" x 6" wooden spacer in the center of the closet door opening on the floor. Install the carpet padding around the block, and install the carpeting over the block. Then attach the closet door guide on top of the carpeted block. This is to keep the door guide from sinking too far into the carpet and padding.

9

Before going any further, check to see if the predrilled doorknob hole and strike plate line up.

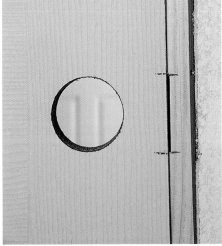

If they do not line up, use shims to enlarge the opening between the door frame and the bottom of the hinged door jamb as necessary. This will raise the doorknob side of the door to meet the doorknob strike plate, as shown.

Holding the bottom of the hinged jamb flush with the drywall, use one No. 8 finish nail and nail just below the shim, straight below the bottom hinge.

Repeat the process on the doorknob side of the jamb. Then shim the door jamb bottom as needed to leave a $1/8$" space between the door jamb and the door.

**13**

Occasionally, the house wall framing may be slightly out of plumb. If so, the door, when shut, may not be flush with the jamb. An easy fix-it trick is to use a shim to protect the jamb and tap the door jambs in the direction needed. You may have to do this on the hinge side as well as the doorknob side.

**14**

When the door is flush with the jamb, use one No. 8 finish nail and nail the hinged jamb just below the top shim, opposite the hinge.

**15**

Use one No. 8 finish nail and nail just below the bottom shim on the hinged jamb, opposite the hinge.

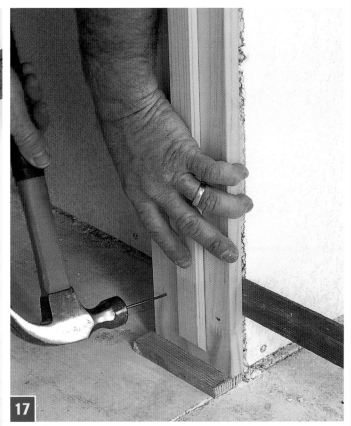

Nail the doorknob side of the jamb just below the bottom shim, opposite the doorknob strike plate.

Nail the doorknob side of the jamb just below the top shim, opposite the doorknob strike plate.

Place a shim between the door frame opening and the hinged jamb just below the top hinge. Adjust the shim to maintain a $\frac{1}{8}$" gap between the jamb and the door. Nail the jamb just below the shim.

**19**

Place a shim between the door frame opening and the hinged jamb, just below the middle hinge. Adjust the shim to maintain a $\frac{1}{8}$" gap between the jamb and the door. Nail the jamb just below the shim.

**20**

Place a shim between the door frame opening and the doorknob jamb, one-third of the way down the jamb. Adjust the shim to maintain a $\frac{1}{8}$" gap between the jamb and the door. Nail the jamb just below the shim.

**21**

Place a shim between the door frame opening and the doorknob jamb, two-thirds of the way down the jamb. Adjust the shim to maintain a $\frac{1}{8}$" gap between the jamb and the door. Nail the jamb just below the shim.

**22**

Open and shut the door to check for $^1/_8$" clearances and ease of door movement. Adjust shims if necessary.

**23**

Set all No. 8 finish nails.

**24**

Using a utility knife, cut off any excess shingles.

**25**

Cut your door trim at a 45° angle at the shortest point, $\frac{1}{2}$" shorter than the outside corner of the door jamb. Using No. 4 finish nails, nail the trim onto the side jamb and wood frame, maintaining a $\frac{1}{4}$" margin all the way down, as shown in the photo. Repeat this process for the other three sides.

**26**

Measure and cut the outside and the inside top trim at a 45° angle on both ends, then nail it on with No. 4 finish nails. Set all the nails.

**27**

Holding the door in the closed position, attach the vertical door stop to the jamb, $\frac{1}{16}$" away from the door on the hinged jamb.

**28**

Holding the door in the closed position, attach the top door stop to the top jamb, $\frac{1}{16}$" away from the door on the hinge side and tight to the door on the doorknob side.

**29**

Holding the door in the closed position, attach the vertical door stop to the jamb, tight to the door on the doorknob side of the jamb.

## CONSTRUCTION TIPS

▪ Remember to nail the door jamb to the door frame just below the shims, not through the shims. This will allow you to adjust the shims if necessary.

**30**

The finished product looks great.

# CHAPTER ELEVEN

# farm-style door trim

If you are looking for an alternative door trim, this might be the one. It is a little more time-consuming than the standard contemporary type, but will transition your home back to an earlier era. This style of trim can also be used around windows and cased openings between rooms, as well as on exterior windows and doors.

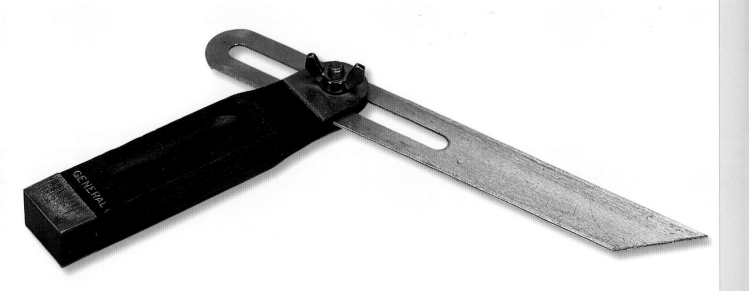

Typically, I use a piece of 1×3 moulding with a bead on one edge. Set the door casing legs with the bead on the door side. Cut the casing $\frac{1}{4}$" longer than the inside corner of the door side jamb and head jamb.

Use $\frac{3}{8}$" × $1\frac{1}{4}$" moulding with a bullnose for the top. Cut this moulding $\frac{3}{8}$" longer on each end than the outside edges of the door casing legs. Before installing, create the bullnose on the ends of the moulding using a rasp or block plane and sand smooth.

Center the moulding to allow a $\frac{3}{8}$" overhang at each door casing leg. Hold the moulding against the wall and nail it to the top of the door casing legs using No. 4 finish nails.

**4**

Cut a piece of 1×5 moulding to the length of the outside edges of each door casing for the head piece. Attach 1³⁄₈" crown moulding to the top edge of the head piece, as shown. Miter the corners of the crown moulding so it will wrap around the head piece.

**5**

## CONSTRUCTION TIPS

▦ If you are trimming doors or windows over paint or wallpaper, you may want to stain your trim pieces prior to installing them.

Place the head piece assembly onto the door casing assembly, aligning the edges of the head piece assembly to the outside edges of the door casing legs. Attach with No. 8 finish nails into the wall studs whenever possible.

# crown moulding

A great way to add a rich and warm touch to your home is the addition of crown moulding. Whether it is painted or stained, the look and feel is hard to beat. Crown moulding can be frustrating to install, but this method works well and cuts down on the frustration.

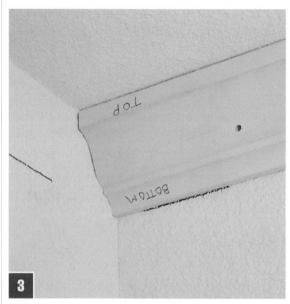

Place the crown moulding upside down on your miter box saw. Adjust it on your saw so that the back side of the crown moulding fits tightly against your fence. Measure the height the crown moulding extends up the fence, and use a pencil to mark the miter box fence at that height.

Cut a small piece of crown moulding to the height it extends up the fence. Using this piece, mark the walls around the ceiling about every 16".

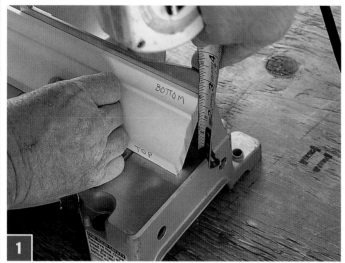

Measure and cut the first piece of crown moulding at a 90° angle from wall to wall and attach it with No. 8 finish nails about every 12". Note: In most cases you do not have to be concerned about finding the framing studs. There should be two 2×4 top wall framing plates to nail into. These plates sit directly on top of the wall frame behind the crown moulding you are installing.

For the second piece of crown moulding, measure from wall to wall. Cut one end of the crown moulding at a 90° angle to fit into the corner opposite the crown moulding you just installed. Measuring from the square end you just cut, mark the bottom of the moulding. Holding the crown moulding upside down in your miter box saw, cut the end that will join the crown moulding already installed, on a 45° angle, with the longest part of the 45° angle at the bottom of the crown moulding.

Using your coping saw, undercut the end of the crown moulding, using the cut you just made as a guideline, as shown in the photo.

Place the crown moulding into position and check the fit.

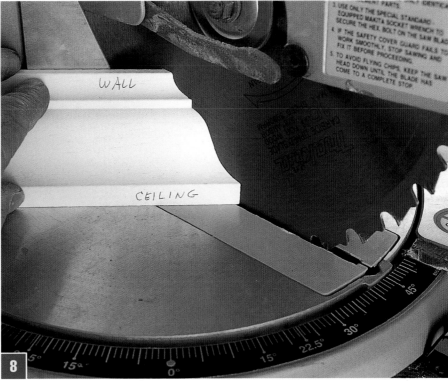

Attach the moulding with No. 8 finish nails about every 12".

For outside corners, measure from the outside corner of the wall to the inside corner of the wall. Hold the crown moulding upside down on your miter box saw and cut a 45° angle, with the shortest point of the cut being at the bottom of the crown moulding.

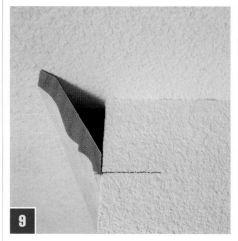

**9**

Attach with No. 8 finish nails
about every 12".

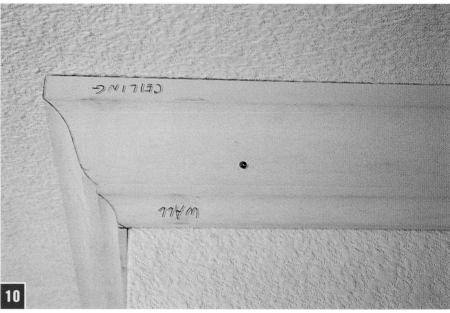

**10**

Cut and attach the next outside crown moulding
using No. 8 finish nails.

## CONSTRUCTION TIPS

▓ Remember to cut the crown moulding in
an upside-down position on your miter saw.
Pretend that the table of your miter saw is the
ceiling and the fence is the wall.

Practice undercutting with a coping saw
on the inside corners. This is the best way to
make a tight-fitting inside corner joint and is
worth the effort! Keep making test cuts on
small pieces of moulding until you have it
figured out. This technique will work on any
type of moulding.

**11**

Using a sanding block, touch up the outside crown moulding corner joints.

No matter what room
you choose, crown
moulding is always
worth the effort.

# CHAPTER THIRTEEN

# closet organizers

One great improvement to any home is to make better use of the storage space. Closet organizers will do just that. In this chapter I will show a quick and inexpensive way to build closet organizers. Once they are completed, you will be amazed at the additional storage and clothing space you will have.

# Building a Stack of Shelves with One Full-Length Top Shelf and Double Closet Poles

**1**

Start by removing the old pole and shelf, and measure the width of the closet to determine the room you have to work with.

**2**

Decide on the arrangement of your organizer. (See step fifteen for some closet arrangement ideas.) Measure the height of the closet to locate the highest shelf. Typically, if you want one pole, the pole is 70" from the floor, and if you want two poles, the poles are set 40" and 80" from the floor.

**3**

For this closet, we have chosen a stack of 20"-wide by 16"-deep shelves and two poles. We will have room for one 12"-deep shelf over the top of the poles and stack of shelves, which means we need a 16" divider, 82" high. Measure 12" in from the top back of the divider and cut off the front corner at a 45° angle, as shown in the photo.

**4**

Determine the shelf spacing you prefer and cut $\frac{1}{2}$"-thick by $1\frac{1}{4}$"-wide shelf support cleats. Glue and nail the cleats using No. 3 finish nails.

**5**

After nailing the shelf support cleats onto the 16" divider, use the divider as a template and stand it up in the closet in the location where it will be installed. Using your pencil, mark the back of the closet wall for the shelf cleat locations. Then move the divider to the side and mark the side wall.

**6**

After cutting the required number of shelf support cleats, glue and nail them to the side wall using No. 8 finish nails.

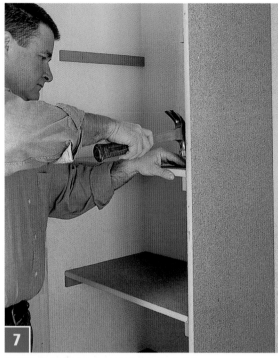

After cutting the 16"-deep by 20"-long closet shelves, nail the shelves to the divider support cleats and the wall support cleats using No. 4 finish nails.

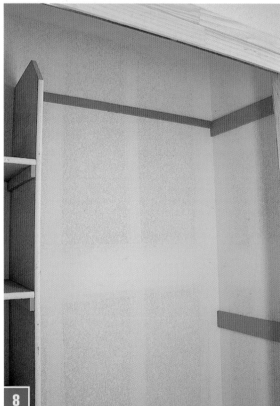

After cutting two ³/₄" × 3" pole support cleats, glue and nail them on the opposite side wall of the closet using No. 8 finish nails. In this case, the tops of the pole support cleats are 41" and 82" off of the floor. Then, measure and cut a shelf support cleat to fit between the top pole support cleat and the shelf divider, as shown.

After measuring and cutting a 12"-deep top shelf that will go from side wall to side wall, place it on top of the shelf support cleats and the shelf support divider. Nail it to the support cleats and the divider using No. 6 finish nails. This will hold the shelf support divider in place.

# Building a Stack of Shelves with Two Full-Length Top Shelves and a Single Closet Pole

10

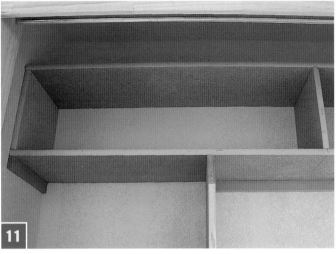

11

In this closet, the shelf support divider is 16"-deep by 72"-tall. After installing the first 12"-deep full-length shelf, cut three 12"-long by 12"-deep pieces of closet shelf for shelf supports. Stand these up and nail them in place at the two sides and middle of the closet using No. 6 finish nails. If your closet is long, add more shelf supports as needed.

After nailing in the 12" × 12" closet shelf supports, cut the second 12"-deep full-length closet shelf and nail it in using No. 6 finish nails.

12

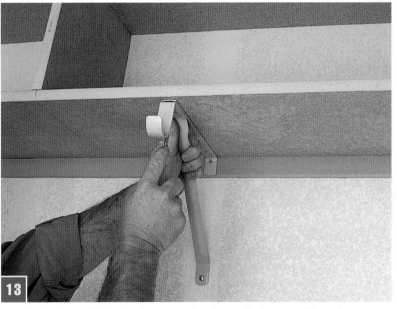

13

Attach the closet shelf and pole support bracket to the bottom of the closet's full-length shelf and to a framing stud in the closet wall, as close to the center of the shelf as possible.

Attach the closet pole holders (rosettes), which can be purchased at a local home-improvement store.

After cutting to length and installing the closet poles, cut and attach the closet baseboard. Note: In this case carpet will be installed in the closet, so I held the baseboard $\frac{3}{8}$" off the floor with spacers.

These are the closet designs that were picked for this home. Using these same design and building techniques, you can easily build inexpensive and sturdy closet organizers that will fit your needs.

As you can see in these photos, the design possibilities for closet organizers are endless. Whether you need more clothing space or more shelf space, simply go to your local home-improvement store, grab some shelving material and go for it.

**16**

## CONSTRUCTION TIPS

▨ You can purchase particle-board shelving material at your local home-improvement store or door shop in standard 12" and 16" widths.

As with any job, the finish is important. I recommend using a good-quality paint-grade caulking to caulk all the joints and seams.

The top coat of finish paint will go on much better if a primer is used to seal the wood first. If necessary, use two coats of primer. Then, paint with semi-gloss paint for a finish that is easy to clean.

# CHAPTER FOURTEEN

# built-in cabinets

I nstalling built-in cabinets is a great way to make the cabinets appear as part of the room.

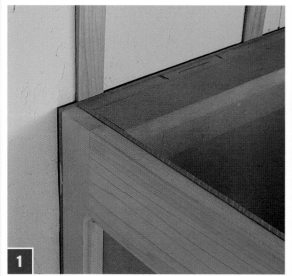

When you install a base cabinet, use shims to plumb and level the cabinet before you screw the cabinet to the wall with $2\frac{1}{2}$" wood screws.

When designing built-in cabinets, build the inside cabinet body $\frac{1}{2}$" smaller than the face frame to allow for any walls that aren't perfectly square, so the face frame will still fit tightly against the wall, as shown.

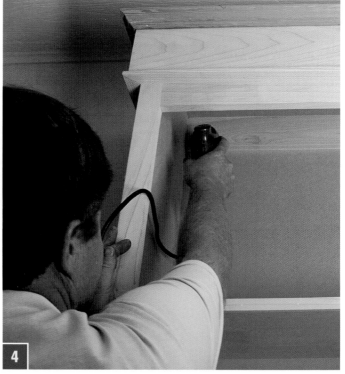

With the base cabinet set in place, set the base top on the base cabinet. Use a pencil to scribe the base top to the wall. Trim the top as necessary.

Predrill holes into the upper cabinet top nailer for $2\frac{1}{2}$" wood screws that will attach the cabinet to the interior wall framing studs. Countersink the screw holes. This allows you to fill the screw holes after you have inserted the screws through the nailer and into the studs.

Cover the gaps between the cabinet and the wall by attaching small strips of moulding.

To achieve a truly custom built-in look, use paintable latex caulking and caulk all gaps and seams as necessary. This is probably one of the most important steps for a paint-finished cabinet, as it creates a seamless fit between the wall and the cabinet.

# More Tricks for Built-in's

This is another way to level cabinets. You can buy a wide variety of cabinet levelers, but they all work basically the same way. Many of them are adjustable at both the foot and from above through an access hole you drill in the cabinet's bottom. This feature is a huge convenience when leveling your cabinet on an uneven floor.

Once the cabinet is level front to back as well as left to right, you can plug the holes you drilled to access the leveler hardware. Many brands of levelers come with their own plastic plugs, though a shop-made tapered wooden plug works just as well.

These illustrations show two methods of fitting built-in cabinets to side walls. The simple fitting strip is attached to a smaller cabinet, the cabinet is leveled, a scribing line is drawn on the strip, the cabinet is pulled away from the wall, the scribe is cut to fit and the cabinet is set in place.

Another solution for a larger cabinet is to glue a narrow backing strip to the cabinet behind the fitting strip. (See illustration for the complex fitting strip.) Then you attach the fitting strip to the backing board using several biscuits but no glue. This allows you to set the cabinet against the wall, mark your scribe, cut it and then put the cabinet in place. Then you fine-tune the fit by pulling the strip out for more trimming.

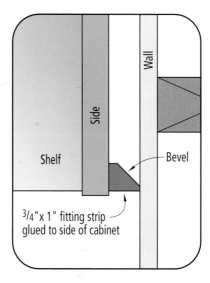

Shelf · Side · Wall · Bevel

3/4"x 1" fitting strip glued to side of cabinet

**Simple fitting strip**
Plan view

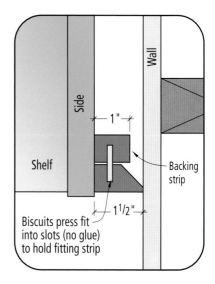

Shelf · Side · Wall · 1" · Backing strip

Biscuits press fit into slots (no glue) to hold fitting strip · 1 1/2"

**Complex fitting strip**
Plan view

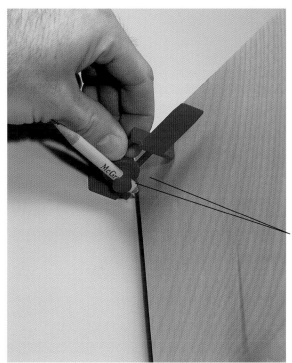

This cabinet has a deep rabbet cut into the back edge of the side (see illustration) to serve as a scribe. To set your scribing tool, use a ruler to find the biggest gap between the back edge of your cabinet side and the wall. Set your scribe to span this distance exactly. Now run the scribing tool up the back edge of your cabinet — being sure to maintain contact with both the wall and cabinet. The pencil will draw your cut line on the back edge of the cabinet side.

**LARGEST GAP BETWEEN WALL AND CABINET**

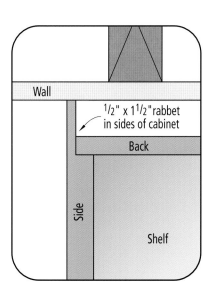

**Back rabbet detail**
Plan view

Wall

$^1/_2$" x $1^1/_2$" rabbet in sides of cabinet

Back

Side

Shelf

**SCRIBE LINE**

After scribing to the wall, lay the cabinet on its side. Many professionals use a belt sander to remove the material down to the scribe line. Belt sanders are a little too speedy for my tastes. I prefer to use a jigsaw to cut right up to the line and then clean up the cut with a block plane. It's still quick, and there's little chance of obliterating your scribe line.

# CHAPTER FIFTEEN

# bag painting

If you are feeling imaginative and would like to dress up a room, hallway or even your whole house, a great way to do so is to experiment with bag painting. It is inexpensive and will give your room a professionally wallpapered look and feel. The hardest part about bag painting is deciding which colors to use. Once you have decided on your colors and started the process, it goes amazingly fast. At the end of the day you can stand back and admire your work.

# getting started

WHAT YOU NEED:

1. Masking tape, paper and paint tarps
2. Standard paint roller
3. Standard paint edger
4. Standard paint roller pan
5. Plastic gloves
6. Plastic grocery bags
7. Three colors of good-quality latex paint (buy two colors of paint; the third color is made by mixing equal parts from the two original colors).

Once you have decided to give bag painting a try, the first step is to mask off anything that you do not want to paint (doors, windows, etc.). Typically, I will mask off about 12" around what I do not want to paint, and protect the floor with a tarp. Then, using a standard paint roller and edger, paint a solid base coat on the walls.

The first or base coat can be light or dark. I recommend a lighter color if you have a small room because a darker color can make a small room appear and feel even smaller. A darker color can be used in a larger room. Your accent colors will be lighter on a dark wall and darker on a light wall. Pour a small amount (about 1 cup) of the second color into the paint roller pan, mixing in about ¼ cup of clean water. When thoroughly mixed, put on your plastic gloves and loosely wad up a plastic grocery bag. Dip it into the paint a little, then dab it on the wall in a circular fashion about 12" apart. Continue this process until the consistency of the dabbing resembles the photo. If you are getting a few paint runs, don't worry; continue the dabbing motion. As the bag dries out, dab over the top of the runs.

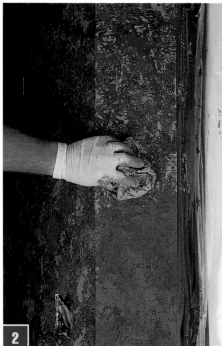

If desired, repeat this process for a third or fourth color of your choice.

If you are doing a major remodel, it is a good idea to do your bag painting before putting on the door trim, window trim and wainscot.

4

No matter what colors you decide upon, bag painting is a great way to dress up any room for the price of a little paint and effort.

## CONSTRUCTION TIPS

▓ Latex paints are available in different sheens, so be creative if you like. For example, use a semigloss for the base coat and a flat sheen for the bagged color for added character.

# project kids toy plans

I've included plans for some of the toys that the kids like to make. Precut the toys to rough shape. Then draw cutting lines on the blanks for the kids to follow to finish cutting out the toys. They then drill, sand, glue and screw the projects together. They also love to decorate the toys after they've assembled them.

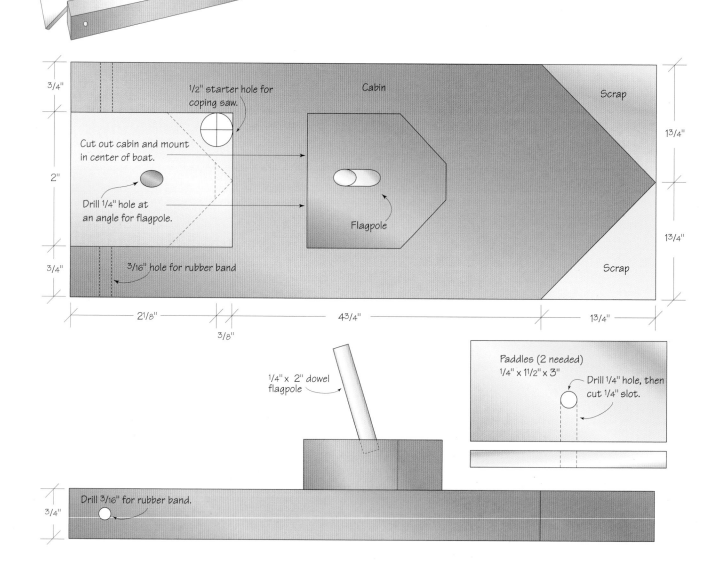

**Speed Boat**

3/4"

1/2" starter hole for coping saw.

Cabin

Scrap

13/4"

Cut out cabin and mount in center of boat.

2"

Flagpole

Drill 1/4" hole at an angle for flagpole.

13/4"

3/4"

3/16" hole for rubber band

Scrap

21/8"

43/4"

13/4"

3/8"

1/4" x 2" dowel flagpole

Paddles (2 needed)
1/4" x 11/2" x 3"

Drill 1/4" hole, then cut 1/4" slot.

Drill 3/16" for rubber band.

3/4"

# Race Car

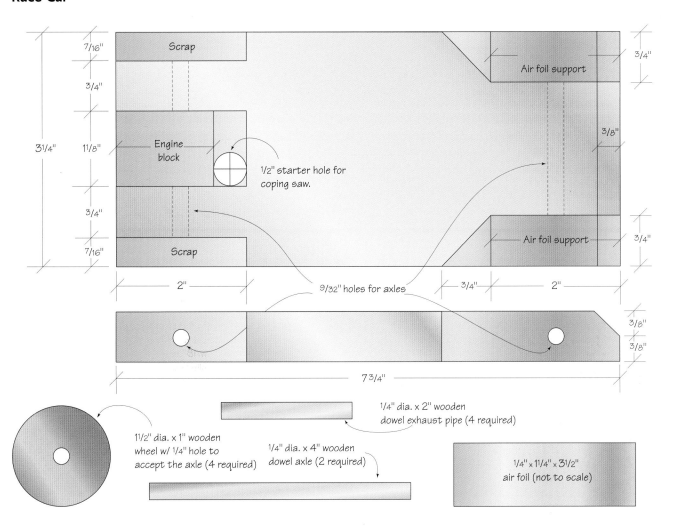

7/16"
3/4"
3 1/4"
1 1/8"
3/4"
7/16"

Scrap
Air foil support
3/4"
3/8"
Engine block
1/2" starter hole for coping saw.
Air foil support
3/4"
Scrap

2"
9/32" holes for axles
3/4"
2"

7 3/4"
3/8"
3/8"

1 1/2" dia. x 1" wooden wheel w/ 1/4" hole to accept the axle (4 required)

1/4" dia. x 2" wooden dowel exhaust pipe (4 required)

1/4" dia. x 4" wooden dowel axle (2 required)

1/4" x 1 1/4" x 3 1/2" air foil (not to scale)

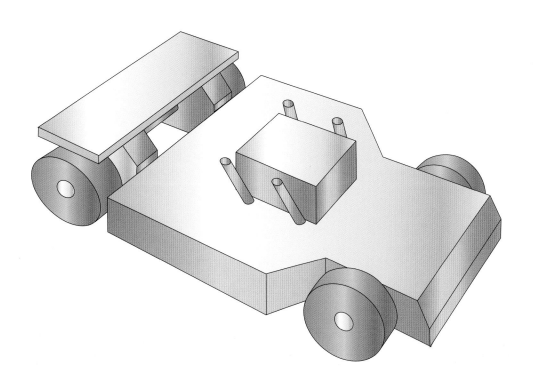

# Birdhouse

All materials 1/2" plywood except for perch.

| | | |
|---|---|---|
| 2-sides | 1/2" x 5" x 8⁵/₈" | |
| 1- front | 1/2" x 4" x 7" | w/ 18° bevel on top edge and 1¹/₂"-diameter hole |
| 1- back | 1/2" x 4" x 8⁵/₈" | w/18° bevel on top edge |
| 1- bottom | 1/2" x 4" x 4" | clip the corners for drainage |
| 1- top | 1/2" x 5" x 6¹/₄" | w/18° bevel on front and back edges |
| 1- perch | ³/₈" x 1³/₄" | wooden dowel |

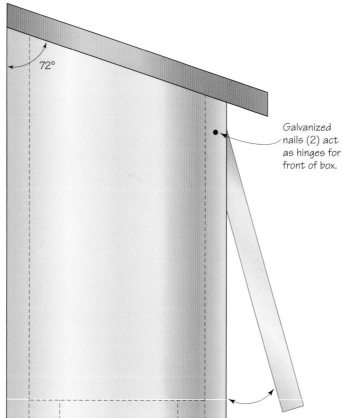

72°

Galvanized nails (2) act as hinges for front of box.

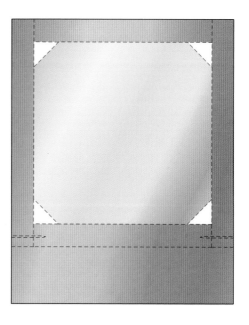

# Drag Racer

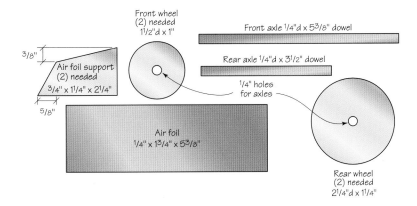

Front wheel
(2) needed
$1^{1/2}$"d x 1"

Front axle $1/4$"d x $5^{3/8}$" dowel

Rear axle $1/4$"d x $3^{1/2}$" dowel

$1/4$" holes
for axles

$3/8$"

Air foil support
(2) needed
$3/4$" x $1^{1/4}$" x $2^{1/4}$"

$5/8$"

Air foil
$1/4$" x $1^{3/4}$" x $5^{3/8}$"

Rear wheel
(2) needed
$2^{1/4}$"d x $1^{1/4}$"

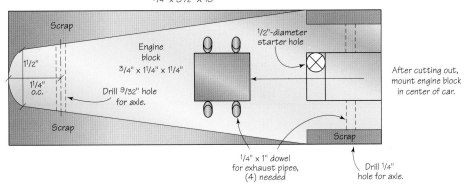

Blank for car body
$3/4$" x $3^{1/2}$" x 10"

Scrap

Engine
block
$3/4$" x $1^{1/4}$" x $1^{1/4}$"

$1/2$"-diameter
starter hole

$1^{1/2}$"

$1^{1/4}$"
o.c.

Drill $9/32$" hole
for axle.

Scrap

Scrap

After cutting out,
mount engine block
in center of car.

$1/4$" x 1" dowel
for exhaust pipes,
(4) needed

Drill $1/4$"
hole for axle.

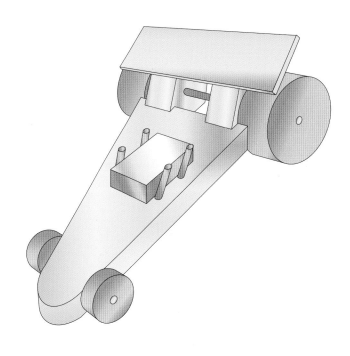

# Rikki's Waddling Duck

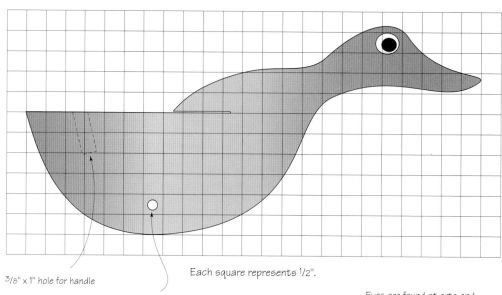

Each square represents ¹/₂".

³/₈" x 1" hole for handle

¹³/₃₂" hole for axle

Eyes are found at arts and crafts store.

Knob is ³/₄" x 1¹/₂"-diameter wheel with ³/₈"-dia. hole.

Handle is ³/₈" x 23¹/₂" dowel rod.

Web feet and wings are thin, black rubber.

4³/₄" x 5¹/₈" web feet

Feet are ³/₄" x 2³/₈"-diameter wheels with slot for web feet and a ³/₈"-dia. hole for the axle.

2" x 3³/₈" web feet (2)

³/₈"-dia. x 2" axle

# appendix

## ▪ COMMON ADHESIVES

| ADHESIVE | ADVANTAGES | DISADVANTAGES | COMMON USES | WORKING TIME | CLAMPING TIME (at 70°F) | CURE TIME | SOLVENT |
|---|---|---|---|---|---|---|---|
| Yellow glue (aliphatic resin) | Easy to use; water resistant; leaves invisible glue lines; economical | Not waterproof (don't use on outdoor furniture) | All-purpose wood glue for interior use; stronger bond than white glue | 5 to 7 minutes | 1 to 2 hours | 24 hours | Warm water |
| Contact cement | Bonds parts immediately | Can't readjust parts after contact; leaves unsightly glue lines | Bonding wood veneer or plastic laminate to substrate | Up to 1 hour | No clamps; parts bond on contact | None | Acetone |
| Superglue (cyanoacrylate) | Bonds parts quickly | Limited to small parts | Bonding small parts made from a variety of materials | 30 seconds | 10 to 60 seconds; clamps usually not required | 30 minutes to several hours | Acetone |
| Epoxy glue | Good gap filler; waterproof; fast-setting formulas available; can be used to bond glass to metal or wood | Requires mixing; expensive; difficult to clean up; very toxic | Bonding small parts made from a variety of materials; bent laminations | 5 to 60 minutes, depending on epoxy formula | 5 minutes to several hours, depending on epoxy formula | 3 hours and longer | Lacquer thinner |
| Animal glue, dry (hide glue) | Extended working time; water cleanup; economical | Must be mixed with water and heated; poor moisture resistance (don't use on outdoor furniture) | Time-consuming assembly work; stronger bond than liquid animal glue; interior use only | 30 minutes | 2 to 3 hours | 24 hours | Warm water |
| Animal glue, liquid (hide glue) | Easy to use; extended working time; economical. | Poor moisture resistance (don't use on outdoor furniture) | Time-consuming assembly work; interior use only | 5 minutes | 2 hours | 24 hours | Warm water |
| Polyurethane | Fully waterproof; gap-filling | Eye and skin irritant | Multipurpose, interior and exterior applications including wood to wood, ceramic, plastic, solid-surface material, stone, metal | 30 minutes | 1 to 2 hours | 8 hours | Mineral spirits while wet; must abrade or scrape off when dry |
| White glue (polyvinyl acetate) | Easy to use; economical | Not waterproof (don't use on outdoor furniture) | All-purpose wood glue for interior use; yellow glue has stronger bond | 3 to 5 minutes | 45 minutes to 2 hours | 24 to 48 hours | Warm water and soap |
| Waterproof glue (resorcinol) | Fully waterproof; extended working time | Requires mixing; dark color shows glue line on most woods; long clamping time | Outdoor furniture, marine applications | 20 minutes | 1 hour | 12 hours | Cool water before hardening |
| Plastic resin (urea-formaldehyde) | Good water resistance; economical | Requires difficult mixing; long clamping time | Outdoor furniture, cutting boards; good for veneering | 15 to 30 minutes | 6 hours | 24 hours | Warm water and soap before hardening |

# COMMON WOODWORKING TERMS

**BEVEL** A cut that is not 90° to a board's face; or the facet left by such a cut.

**BISCUIT** A thin, flat oval of compressed beech that is inserted between two pieces of wood into mating saw kerfs made by a biscuit or plate joining machine.

**BRIDLE JOINT** A joint that combines features of both lap joints and mortise and tenon. It has a U-shaped mortise in the end of the board.

**BUTT JOINT** Two flat facets of mating parts that fit flush together with no interlocking joinery.

**CARPENTER'S GLUE** White and yellow adhesives formulated for use with wood.

**CASING** The trim framing a window, door or other opening.

**CHALK LINE** Line made by snapping a chalk-coated string against a plane.

**CHECK** A crack in wood material caused by drying, either just in the surface or in the ends of the board so the fibers have separated.

**COMPOUND MITER** A cut where the blade path is not perpendicular to the wood's end or edge and the blade tilt is not 90° to the face.

**COPING** Sawing a negative profile in one piece to fit the positive profile of another, usually in moulding.

**COUNTERBORE** A straight-sided drilled hole that recesses a screw head below the wood surface so a wood plug can cover it, or the bit that makes this hole.

**COUNTERSINK** A cone-shaped drilled hole whose slope angle matches the underside of a flat screw head and sinks it flush with the wood surface, or the tool that makes this hole.

**CROSSCUT** To saw wood perpendicular to the grain.

**CUPPING** A drying defect where one side of the board shrinks more across the grain than the other, causing the board to curl in on itself like a trough.

**DADO** A flat-bottomed, U-shaped milling cut of varying widths and depths but always running across the grain.

**DOVETAIL JOINT** A traditional joint characterized by interlocking fingers and pockets shaped like its name. It has exceptional resistance to tension.

**DOWEL** A small cylinder of wood that is used to reinforce a wood joint.

**DRESSING** The process of turning rough lumber into a smooth board with flat, parallel faces and straight, parallel edges and whose edges are square to the face.

**EDGE LAP** A notch that is cut into the edge of a board halfway across its width and that forms half of an edge lap joint.

**FINGERLAP** Lap joint that has straight, interwoven fingers; also called a box joint.

**FINISH** Varnish, stain, paint or any mixture that protects a surface.

**FLAT-SAWN** The most common cut of lumber, where the growth rings run predominantly across the end of the board; or its characteristic grain pattern.

**FLUSH** Level with an adjoining surface.

**GRAIN PATTERN** The visual appearance of wood grain. Types of grain pattern include flat, straight, curly, quilted, rowed, mottled, crotch, cathedral, bee's-wing or bird's-eye.

**HARDWOOD** Wood from broadleaf deciduous trees, no matter what the density (balsa is a hardwood).

**HEARTWOOD** Wood from the core of a tree, usually darker and harder than newer wood.

**JIG** A shop-made or aftermarket device that assists in positioning and steadying the wood or tools.

**JOINTING** The process of making a board face straight and flat or an edge straight, whether by hand or machine.

**KERF** The visible path of subtracted wood left by a saw blade.

**KEY** An inserted joint-locking device, usually made of wood.

**KNOCKDOWN JOINT** A joint that is assembled without glue and can be disassembled and reassembled if necessary.

**LAP JOINT** A type of joint made by removing half the thickness or width of the parts and lapping them over each other.

**LENGTH JOINT** A joint that makes one longer wood unit out of two shorter ones by joining them end to end.

**LEVEL** Absolutely horizontal.

**MILLING** The process of removing material to leave a desired positive or negative profile in the wood.

**MITER** A generic term meaning mainly an angled cut across the face grain, or specifically a 45° cut across the face, end grain or along the grain. See also *bevel*.

**MORTISE** The commonly rectangular or round pocket into which a mating tenon is inserted. Mortises can be blind (stop inside the wood thickness), through or open on one end.

**PARTICLEBOARD** A panel made of wood particles and glue.

**PILOT HOLE** A small, drilled hole used as a guide and pressure relief for screw insertion, or to locate additional drilling work like countersinking and counterboring.

**PLUMB** Absolutely vertical.

**PLYWOOD** Panel made by laminating layers of wood.

**QUARTER-SAWN** A stable lumber cut where the growth rings on the board's end run more vertically across the end than horizontally and the grain on the face looks straight; also called straight-grained or rift-sawn.

**RABBET** A milled cut that leaves a flat step parallel to, but recessed from, the wood's surface.

**RAIL** One of the horizontal parts of a door frame.

**RIP** To cut parallel to the grain of a board.

**SAPWOOD** The new wood in a tree, located between the core (heartwood) and bark. Usually lighter in color.

**SCARF JOINT** A joint that increases the overall length of wood by joining two pieces at their ends, commonly by gluing together two unusually long bevels in their faces or edges.

**SCRIBE** To make layout lines or index marks using a knife or awl.

**SHOULDER** A perpendicular face of a step cut that bears against a mating joint part to stabilize the joint.

**SOFTWOOD** Wood from coniferous evergreen trees, no matter what the density (yew is a softwood).

**SPLINE** A flat, thin strip of wood that fits into mating grooves between two parts to reinforce the joint between them.

**STAIN** A pigment or dye used to color wood through saturation; or a discoloration in wood from fungus or chemicals.

**STILE** One of the vertical parts of a frame.

**TENON** The male part of a mortise-and-tenon joint, commonly rectangular or round, but not restricted to those shapes.

**TONGUE AND GROOVE** Joinery method in which one board is cut with a protruding tongue and another is cut with a matching groove along its edge.

**TWISTING** A drying defect in lumber that causes it to twist so the faces at each end of the board are in a different plane.

**VENEER** A thin sheet of wood bonded to another material.

**WIDTH JOINT** A joint that makes a unit of the parts by joining them edge to edge to increase the overall width of wood.

# ▪ COMMON STAINS AND TOP COATS

## Stains

| STAIN TYPE | FORM | PREPARATION | CHARACTERISTICS |
|---|---|---|---|
| *Pigment Stains* | | | |
| Oil-based | Liquid | Mix thoroughly. | Apply with rag, brush or spray; resists fading. |
| Water-based | Liquid | Mix thoroughly. | Apply with rag, brush or spray; resists fading; water cleanup. |
| Gel | Gel | Ready to use. | Apply with rag; won't raise grain; easy to use; no drips or runs. |
| Water-based gel | Gel | Ready to use. | Apply with rag; easy to use; no drips or runs. |
| Japan color | Concentrated liquid | Mix thoroughly. | Used for tinting stains, paints, varnish, lacquer. |
| *Dye Stains* | | | |
| Water-based | Powder | Mix with water. | Apply with rag, brush or spray; deep penetrating; best resistance of dye stains; good clarity; raises grain. |
| Oil-based | Powder | Mix with toluol, lacquer thinner, turpentine or naphtha. | Apply with rag, brush or spray; penetrating; does not raise grain; dries slowly. |
| Alcohol-based | Powder | Mix with alcohol. | Apply with rag, brush or spray; penetrating; does not raise grain; dries quickly; lap marks sometimes a problem. |
| NGR | Liquid | Mix thoroughly. | Apply with rag, brush or spray (use retarder if wiping or brushing); good clarity; does not raise grain. |

## Top Coats

| FINISH TYPE | FORM | PREPARATION | CHARACTERISTICS | DRY TIME |
|---|---|---|---|---|
| Shellac | Liquid | Mix thoroughly. | Dries quickly; economical; available either clear or amber-colored; high gloss luster; affected by water, alcohol and heat. | 2 hours |
| Shellac flakes | Dry flakes | Mix with alcohol. | Dries quickly; economical (mix only what is needed); color choices from amber to clear; high gloss luster; affected by water, alcohol and heat. | 2 hours |
| Lacquer | Liquid | Mix with thinner for spraying. | Dries quickly; clear (shaded lacquers available); high gloss luster, but flattening agents available; durable; moisture resistant. | 30 minutes |
| Varnish | Liquid | Mix thoroughly. | Dries slowly; amber color; gloss, semigloss and satin lusters; very good durability and moisture resistance; flexible. | 3 to 6 hours |
| Polyurethane | Liquid | Mix thoroughly. | Dries slowly; clear to amber colors; gloss, semigloss and satin lusters; excellent durability and moisture resistance; flexible. | 3 to 6 hours |
| Water-based polyurethane | Liquid | Mix thoroughly. | Dries quickly; clear; won't yellow; gloss and satin lusters; moisture and alcohol resistant; low odor. | 2 hours |
| Tung oil | Liquid | Ready to use. | Dries slowly; amber color; satin luster; poor moisture resistance; easy to use. | 20 to 24 hours |
| Danish oil | Liquid | Mix thoroughly. | Dries slowly; amber color; satin luster; poor moisture resistance; easy to use. | 8 to 10 hours |

**NOTE:** Dry times are based on a temperature of 70° Fahrenheit and 40-percent relative humidity. Lower temperature and/or higher relative humidity can increase drying time.

# WOOD COLOR GUIDE

| COLOR | WOOD | COST | NOTES |
| --- | --- | --- | --- |
| White | Aspen | $ | Soft and easily worked. Can have streaks of brown. |
| | Silver maple | $$ | Hard; stable. Machines and takes finish well. |
| | Spruce (Adirondack spruce, blue spruce, skunk spruce) | $ | Soft and easily worked. Grain has a strong character. |
| | Eastern white pine | $ | Pines have high pitch content that can ruin blades; use blade lubricant. Soft and easy to work but can split. |
| | Sugar pine | $$ | Close, consistent grain. Soft; easy to work. Carves well. |
| | Western white pine | $ | See above for Eastern white pine. |
| | Holly | $$$ | Discolors if the wood is not cut properly. Very nice white color. |
| | Basswood (American lime) | $ | Turns pale brown on exposure. Soft; closed grain. Carves well. |
| | Hard maple (rock maple, sugar maple) | $$ | Hard; stable. Machines and takes finish well. |
| | European ash (English/French/etc. ash) | $$ | Turns light brown on exposure. Machines well. |
| Black | Black walnut | $$ | Medium hard and can be carved. Turns reddish brown over time. |
| | Wenge | $$$ | Hard; brittle. Nice brown color but dust is very irritating. |
| | South American walnut | $$$ | Light brown; medium hardness. Machines well. |
| | Ebony (gaboon) | $$$ | Hard; endangered. Browns to black. Good accent wood. |
| Red | Bloodwood (Brazil redwood, cardinal wood, pau rainha) | $$$ | Nice red color; hard; brittle. Holds color. |
| | Aromatic cedar (Eastern red cedar, chest cedar, Tennessee cedar) | $ | Reddish brown knots with whitish wood. Splits easily; lots of resin in the knots. If finished it loses its aroma. |
| | Cherry | $$ | Medium hard; can be carved. Turns deep brownish red. |
| | Jarrah | $$ | Moderately difficult to work. Takes finish well. |
| | Brazilwood (pernambuco wood, Bahia wood, para wood) | $$$ | Hard; brittle; deep reddish brown colors. |
| | African padauk (camwood, barwood) | $$ | Medium hard; brittle. Turns burgundy color. Dust is irritating. |
| | Redheart | $$$ | Rich red color; medium hard; brittle. Machines well. Holds color. |
| Yellow | Pau amarillo | $$ | Brightest; canary yellow. |
| | Orange osage | $$ | Turns orange-brown on exposure. |
| | Yellow cedar (Alaska cedar, nootka cypress, yellow cypress) | $$ | Soft; easy to work. Carves easily. Usually has nice straight grain. |
| | Yellow pine | $ | Hard, heavy, tough and very strong grain pattern. |
| | Ponderosa pine (Western yellow pine, Californian white pine) | $ | Hard, heavy, tough and very strong grain pattern. |
| | Caragana | $ | Actually a shrub; have to look for it. |
| | Hickory | $$ | Hard; light brown to brown. Bends well. Brittle; heavy. |
| | Yellowheart | $$ | Hard. Holds color fairly well. |
| | Satinwood (East Indian satinwood) | $$$ | Hard; somewhat brittle; moderately difficult to work. |
| | Obeche (ayous, wawa, arere) | $ | Hard; somewhat brittle; moderately difficult to work. |
| Green | Staghorn sumac (velvet sumac) | $ | Difficult to find. |
| | American yellow poplar (tulip tree, canary wood, canoe wood) | $ | Medium hard; light brown, green and purple. Machines well. |
| | Vera wood (Maracaibo, lignum vitae, guyacan) | $$$ | Hard; oily; close grain. Machines well. |
| Blue/Gray | Spruce (Adirondack spruce, blue spruce, skunk spruce) | $ | Some spruce boards have gray or blue cast. |
| | Blue mahoe (mahoe, mountain mahoe, seaside mahoe) | $$$ | Heartwood varies from purple, metallic blue, olive brown. Must search for blue. |
| Purple | Purpleheart (violet wood, pauroxo, coracy) | $$ | Hard; brittle. Dust is irritating. Holds color well. |
| Orange | Orange osage | $$ | Cuts yellow, then turns orange on exposure; medium hard. |
| | Zebrawood | $$$ | Dark streaks throughout. Soft; splits easily; good accent wood. |
| | Red gum (sweet gum, alligator wood, hazel pine) | $$ | Streaks of red and black; beautiful grain; good accent wood. |

Legend:
**$** Free or inexpensive
**$$** Moderately priced
**$$$** Expensive

# suppliers

**ADAMS & KENNEDY – THE WOOD SOURCE**
6178 Mitch Owen Road
P.O. Box 700
Manotick, Ontario, Canada K4M 1A6
613-822-6800
www.wood-source.com
*Wood supply*

**AIR HANDLING SYSTEMS (MANUFACTURERS
SERVICE CO., INC.)**
5 Lunar Drive
Woodbridge, Connecticut 06525-2320
800-367-3828
www.airhand.com
*Dust collector ductwork and fittings*

**BALL AND BALL**
463 West Lincoln Highway
Exton, Pennsylvania 19341
800-257-3711
www.ballandball-us.com
*Hardware reproductions*

**BIESEMEYER WOODWORKING TOOLS**
216 South Alma School Road, Suite 3
Mesa, Arizona 85210
800-782-1831
www.biesemeyer.com
*Fences, guards, splitters*

**CONSTANTINES WOOD CENTER**
1040 East Oakland Park Boulevard
Fort Lauderdale, Florida 33334
954-561-1716
www.constantines.com
*Tools, woods, veneers, hardware*

**CMT USA, INC.**
307-F Pomona Drive
Greensboro, North Carolina 27407
888-268-2487
www.cmtusa.com
*Cove cutter, carbide-tipped tooling*

**DELTA MACHINERY**
P.O. Box 2468
Jackson, Tennessee 38302-2468
800-223-7278 (U.S.)
800-463-3582 (Canada)
www.deltawoodworking.com
*Woodworking tools*

**DOUG MOCKETT & COMPANY, INC.**
P.O. Box 3333
Manhattan Beach, California 90266
800-523-1269 (U.S. & Canada)
310-381-2491 (outside of the U.S. & Canada)
www.mockett.com
*Computer furniture accessory hardware*

**ECOGATE, INC.**
1821 Tyburn Street
Glendale, California 91204
888-326-4283
www.ecogate.com
*Dust collection systems*

**EXAKTOR PRECISION WOODWORKING TOOLS, INC.**
4 Glenbourne Park
Markham, Ontario, Canada L6C 1G9
800-387-9789
www.exaktortools.com
*Accessories for the table saw*

**SUPPLIERS,** continued

**FORREST MANUFACTURING COMPANY, INC.**
461 River Road
Clifton, New Jersey 07014
800-733-7111
forrest.woodmall.com
*Carbide-tipped saw blades, dado sets,*
*sharpening*

**FREUD TOOLS**
218 Feld Avenue
High Point, North Carolina 27263
800-334-4107
www.freudtools.com
*Carbide-tipped saw blades, dado sets, tooling*

**GARRETT WADE**
161 Avenue of the Americas
New York, New York 10013
800-221-2942
www.garrettwade.com
*General hand tools and supplies, some*
*power tools*

**THE HOME DEPOT**
2455 Paces Ferry Road
Atlanta, Georgia 30339
770-433-8211 (U.S.)
800-668-2266 (Canada)
www.homedepot.com
*Tools, paint, wood, electrical, garden*

**HATTERAS HAMMOCKS**
P.O. Box 1602
Greenville, North Carolina 27835
800-643-3522
www.hatham.com
*Hammocks*

**HORTON BRASSES, INC.**
Nooks Hill Road
PO Box 95
Cromwell, Connecticut 06416
800-754-9127
www.horton-brasses.com
*Hardware for antique furniture; Hepplewhite,*
*Chippendale and Victorian brass hardware;*
*hand-forged iron hardware*

**HOUSE OF TOOLS LTD.**
100 Mayfield Common Northwest
Edmonton, Alberta, Canada T5P 4B3
800-661-3987
www.houseoftools.com
*Woodworking tools and hardware*

**THE JAPAN WOODWORKER CATALOG**
1731 Clement Avenue
Alameda, California 94501
800-537-7820
www.japanwoodworker.com
*Traditional Japanese hand tools; some*
*general tools; books*

**JESSEM TOOL COMPANY**
171 Robert T. E. # 7 & # 8
Penetanguishene, Ontario, Canada L9M 1G9
800-436-6799
www.jessem.com
*Rout-R-Slide and Rout-R-Lift*

**KLINGSPOR'S WOODWORKING SHOP**
P.O. Box 5069
Hickory, North Carolina 28603-5069
800-228-0000
www.woodworkingshop.com
*Tools and supplies*

**LEE VALLEY TOOLS LTD.**
U.S.:
P.O. Box 1780
Ogdensberg, New York 13669-6780
800-267-8735
Canada:
P.O. Box 6295, Station J
Ottawa, Ontario, Canada K2A 1T4
800-267-8761
www.leevalley.com
*Fine woodworking tools and hardware*

**LOCKWOOD PRODUCTS, INC.**
5615 Southwest Willow Lane
P.O. Box 1546
Lake Oswego, Oregon 97035
800-423-1625
www.loc-line.com
*Loc-Line modular hose*

**LOWE'S HOME IMPROVEMENT WAREHOUSE**
P.O. Box 1111
North Wilkesboro, North Carolina 28656
800-445-6937
www.lowes.com
*Tools, paint, wood, electrical, garden*

**LRH ENTERPRISES**
9250 Independence Avenue
Chatsworth, California 91311
800-423-2544
www.lrhent.com
*Magic Molder*

**ONEIDA AIR SYSTEMS, INC.**
1001 West Fayette Street
Syracuse, New York 13204
800-732-4065
www.oneida-air.com
*Dust collectors*

**PACKARD WOODWORKS, INC.**
P.O. Box 718
Tryon, North Carolina 28782
800-683-8876
www.packardwoodworks.com
*Woodturning supplies*

**PAXTON WOODCRAFTERS' STORE**
4837 Jackson Street
Denver, Colorado 80216
800-332-1331
www.paxton-woodsource.com
*Domestic and foreign hardwoods; veneers; books and woodworking tools*

**PORTER-CABLE**
4825 Highway 45 North
P.O. Box 2468
Jackson, Tennessee 38302-2468
800-487-8665
www.porter-cable.com
*Woodworking tools*

**RICHELIEU HARDWARE**
7900 West Henri-Bourassa
Ville St-Laurent, Quebec, Canada H4S 1V4
800-619-5446 (U.S.)
800-361-6000 (Canada)
www.richelieu.com
*Hardware supplies*

**ROCKLER WOODWORKING AND HARDWARE**
4365 Willow Drive
Medina, Minnesota  55340
800-279-4441
www.rockler.com
*Woodworking tools and hardware*

**SEVEN CORNERS HARDWARE, INC.**
216 West 7th Street
St. Paul, Minnesota 55102
651-224-4859
www.7cornershdwe.com
*Discount mail order; mostly power tools*

**SIKKENS WOOD CARE PRODUCTS**
1845 Maxwell Street
Troy, Michigan 48084
800-833-7288
www.sikkens.com
*Wood finishes*

SUPPLIERS, continued

**TENRYU AMERICA, INC.**
7964 Kentucky Drive, Suite 12
Florence, Kentucky 41042
800-951-7297
www.tenryu.com
*Saw blades*

**TOOL CRIB OF THE NORTH**
P.O. Box 14930
Grand Forks, North Dakota 58208-4930
800-358-3096
www.amazon.com/toolcrib
*Discount mail-order power tools*

**TOOL TREND LTD.**
140 Snow Boulevard
Concord, Ontario, Canada L4K 4C1
416-663-8665
*Woodworking tools and hardware*

**VAN DYKE'S RESTORERS**
P.O. Box 278
39771 S.D. Highway 34
Woonsocket, South Dakota 57385
800-558-1234
www.vandykes.com
*Supplies for upholstery and antique restoration; antique reproduction hardware*

**VAUGHAN & BUSHNELL MANUFACTURING**
11414 Maple Avenue
Hebron, Illinois 60034
815-648-2446
www.vaughanmfg.com
*Hammers and other tools*

**WILKE MACHINERY COMPANY**
3230 North Susquehanna Trail
York, Pennsylvania 17402-9716
800-235-2100
www.wilkemach.com
*Woodworking tools*

**WOLFCRAFT NORTH AMERICA**
1222 West Ardmore Avenue
P.O. Box 687
Itasca, Illinois 60143
630-773-4777
www.wolfcraft.com
*Woodworking hardware and accessories*

**WOOD CARVERS SUPPLY, INC.**
P.O. Box 7500
Englewood, Florida 34295-7500
800-284-6229
www.woodcarverssupply.com
*Carving tools and supplies*

**WOODCRAFT**
P.O. Box 1686
Parkersburg, West Virginia 26102-1686
800-225-1153
www.woodcraft.com
*Woodworking hardware and accessories*

**THE WOODTURNERS CATALOG**
Craft Supplies USA
1287 East 1120 South
Provo, Utah 84606
800-551-8876
www.woodturnerscatalog.com
*Woodturning supplies*

**WOODWORKER'S HARDWARE**
P.O. Box 180
Sauk Rapids, Minnesota 56379-0180
800-383-0130
www.wwhardware.com
*Woodworking tools and accessories; finishing supplies; books and plans*

**WOODWORKER'S SUPPLY**
1108 North Glenn Road
Casper, Wyoming 82601
800-645-9292
www.woodworker.com
*Woodworking tools and accessories; finishing supplies; books and plans*

# index

# The best woodworking projects come from
# Popular Woodworking Books!

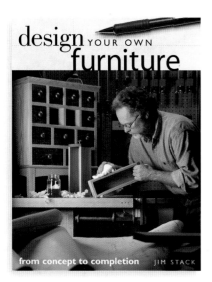

From beds to bookcases, this book provides all the instruction, advice and photos you need to master furniture design techniques with confidence. Jim Stack details everything from roughing out your initial concept to creating an accurate cutting list. You'll learn how to determine which design elements, materials, and joinery techniques are right for the piece you have in mind.

ISBN 1-55870-613-5, paperback, 128 pages, #70555-K

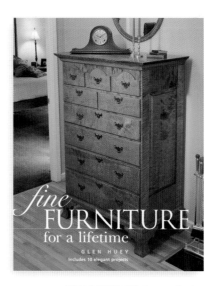

Make the most of your time in the shop by creating furniture pieces friends and family will marvel over for years to come! Glen Huey provides easy-to-follow instructions and step-by-step photos for ten exciting projects inspired by 18th- and 19th- century designs. You'll learn how to craft gorgeous furniture with classic lines and solid construction.

ISBN 1-55870-593-7, paperback, 128 pages, #70533-K

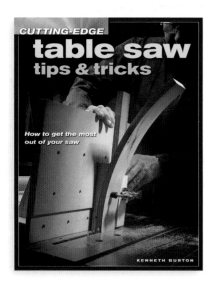

Ken Burton illustrates just how important and efficient your table saw can be with dozens of tricks, techniques and jigs that cover the entire range of what a table saw can do. Everything from crafting precision joinery to accurately cutting pieces to size. Each technique is easy-to-do, safe to execute, and certain to save you time and money.

ISBN 1-55870-623-2, paperback, 128 pages, #70569-K

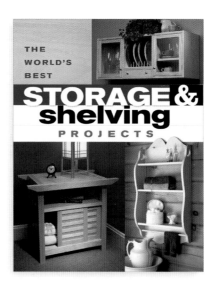

Make the most of your time in the woodshop by building the best projects available! Inside you'll find 18 of the most requested storage and shelving projects from the pages of *Popular Woodworking* magazine. From basic shelves to high-end bookcases, each project comes with easy-to-follow instructions, step-by-step photos, technical drawings and cutting lists.

ISBN 1-55870-639-9, paperback, 128 pages, #70587-K